THE COMPLETE BOOK OF
INTERNATIONAL
SMUGGLING

M.C. FINN

THE COMPLETE BOOK OF
INTERNATIONAL
SMUGGLING

PALADIN PRESS
BOULDER, COLORADO

The Complete Book of International Smuggling
by M. C. Finn
Copyright © 1983 by M. C. Finn

ISBN 0-87364-268-6
Printed in the United States of America

Published by Paladin Press, a division of
Paladin Enterprises, Inc., P.O. Box 1307,
Boulder, Colorado 80306, USA.
(303) 443-7250

Direct inquiries and/or orders to the above address.

Two photos in this book were used with permission of World Wide Photos.

Contents

To Myles

In the early evening darkness, the rain begins . . .
a phosphorous wake vanishes astern
stars alone light the way . . .
We draw near
one word is spoken, another heard
on board, torn money is reunited
A chute is lowered
an avalanche of bales fill the deck
Low in the water we return . . .

The Smoker's Guide to the Florida Keys

*We trained hard . . . but every time
we were beginning to form up into teams,
we would be reorganized. I was to learn
later in life that we tend to meet any
new situation by reorganizing . . . and a
wonderful method it can be for creating
the illusion of progress while producing
inefficiency and demoralization.*

Petronius, A.D. 66

1. Destination America

SMUGGLING OF CONTRABAND TO the Western World is the largest business on this earth. If one were to add up the profits obtained from all illegal smuggling operations to all the countries of this earth, the money would more than triple all the profits of America's Fortune 500 companies. We are a smuggling people. The profits are enormous, and risks of detection are minimal.

On a recent business trip abroad, I talked with a well-to-do executive in the airplane's first-class cabin. He worked for an oil company and was on his way home. On his wrist was an $8,000 gold Rolex watch. I admired the watch as I spoke with the business executive. During our conversation, he told me that he had a *connection* in Switzerland where he buys the watches for $3,150 U.S. currency. He buys three every trip and sells them to his cousin (a jeweler) for $4,500 apiece. His cousin then sells them to the public for $7,500 apiece. The executive makes $4,050 profit each trip. The jeweler buys the watches and makes a cool $9,000 profit. Never are duties paid, nor are the watches declared when he is entering the United States. He puts one on his wrist and the others in his coat pocket. This executive is one of the leaders of a large U.S. company, a college graduate,

1

and a pillar of his community. In his mind he is only playing a game, a harmless game. Since he may make ten to fifteen trips a year abroad, his tax-free profits on watches alone are between $40,000 and $60,000. He calls it play money.

Just how many executives who travel fit this mold is unknown, but the guess is thousands of $60,000-plus executives are small-time play money smugglers. We are not talking of drugs, but rather of everything from French perfume to Japanese tablecloths, from Rolex watches to designer jeans. Besides the real name brand goods, tons of counterfeit materials reach our shores each day. If this executive had a good connection in Hong Kong, he could buy good Rolex counterfeits for only $100 apiece. With a third world connection this executive could have sold the counterfeits for $2,000 to $3,000 apiece. A cool profit to say the least. This is done every day, seven days a week. More counterfeit watches, jeans, wines, tablecloths, jewelry, and other items are sold every day than originals. This is big business, and it is run by legitimate businessmen. Many undertake this enterprise as a second business, and many retire rich. For every real or legitimate item there is a counterfeit brother and in many cases several counterfeit brothers.

Our business executive friend does not believe he is *smuggling* goods—only making play money. In essence, smuggling is the free enterprise system working at its best.

Who makes this system work? Well, everyone from politicians to the police. Payoffs, *mordida,* and other graft are a way of life. What constitutes smuggling depends on where you are and how the law is interpreted there. What is considered smuggling in the United States may not be smuggling in Guatemala.

We spoke with a German once who makes his living building and smuggling cars. These specially made cars were designed to carry Bibles into Russia and other Eastern European countries. Bibles are a "no no" in the Soviet Union. A large Baptist church in Miami sponsored this operation, and according to our sources some members of this smuggling operation have been caught, killed or jailed by Russian authorities. Is this illegal? Maybe not in God's eyes, but Mr. Andropov seems to frown on it. How can Bible smuggling be good and Rolex smuggling be bad? Well, this is a difficult question and depends on whether you're after profits or souls; but whatever your answer, it shows even ministers support smuggling operations.

In Eastern Europe one cannot own Bibles. In most other areas on earth one can have Bibles. When one crosses into Eastern Europe with Bibles he or she becomes a smuggler, and is then subject to years in prison. By Western standards he is persecuted; by Eastern standards he is a criminal smuggler.

In Russia, it is illegal to take icons out of the country. In Western Europe and most other areas of the world it is perfectly legal to bring icons into the country. Hence in Russia one who takes out icons is a smuggler. When he arrives in the Western European country, he is only an immigrant or importer.

It is perfectly legal to buy televisions and other electrical appliances in the United States. When you load these electrical items on a DC-3 airplane and fly to Mexico you have now broken the law and are a smuggler. This is done every day, seven days a week.

If one travels to the state of North Carolina and buys 100 cases of cigarettes and then drives to Utah and sells them to a friend, they are both smugglers.

Rubies and emeralds are legal in Thailand and

Colombia, but the second you don't pay Uncle Sam huge duties and you cross into America you are a smuggler.

Smuggling is the second oldest profession on the earth. Basically, it is a supply and demand business or the free enterprise system at its finest. Since smugglers forget to pay revenue on their import or export item, the government receives no revenue. It is this revenue that the government wants very badly. The opposition to smuggling centers on government's "lost dollars."

In America our government can send 55,000 boys to their death in Vietnam and nothing will happen. Billions of our tax dollars are totally wasted by bureaucrats and we as a country go deeper and deeper in debt. But forget to pay taxes one year on cash earned and you are a violator and must go to jail so others can be protected.

One must realize that smuggling is much like our life in Vietnam. There are rules that must be followed for success. Get too careless and you fall. Perhaps America's best smuggling groups are run by former military veterans. They are patriotic and honest. But their one failure is to give payments to the government on cash earned.

One banker in New York recently told me that we in the United States are in for some bad economic times and that soon only smugglers will be in the black ink. He went on to say how his bank was dodging certain treasury laws because banking is competitive and only the slightly corrupt will survive these troubled times.

Every businessman uses some deceptive tactics. The bottom line is profits. It should be fully understood that almost all businessmen, politicians, and police are in a sense not only deceptive, but conspirators in the world of intrigue and smuggling. This business touches all of us, from the housewife to the executive, from the minister to the college professor. No one is immune, and no one is left untouched by the effects of the smuggling operational system.

We should now take a serious look at how to be a businessman smuggler. How does one avoid inspection, and how does the executive set up such an operation?

First, look at the areas you are going to in your foreign travel and identify just what you might be able to import. If you decide on watches as our executive friend did, then find a connection who will buy the material. Most independent jewelers or your local gold and silver exchange will purchase legitimate watches at low prices. After all, everyone wants to turn a profit. Discount jewelers often scoff at these items, but sometimes the best market of all is the large local flea market. Just rent a table and put out your items. Not all of them, just a sample. You'll be surprised at how many people want them. We recommend south Florida markets for jewelry, watches, parrots, other exotic birds, and paintings. Yes, paintings sell quite as well as diamonds and watches. New York and Los Angeles are also good markets. Lots of cash is available in south Florida and Los Angeles for these items. The flea markets in Fort Lauderdale and Miami are very good. Just check your local listings and you'll easily get started.

For wild birds, look for "Bird Distributor" in the Yellow Pages. Miami is the center of this action, and most stores or dealers there will help with any paperwork the government requires. There are many independent quarantine centers, and this process is necessary to ensure the health of the animal. Use only the independent centers, because most of the dealers there will be helpful.

Always make a dry run to check your people out. Snitches are all over Miami, so to protect yourself and your product, make several dry runs first. You must know what a snitch is—a whore who sells his soul to law enforcement agencies anywhere for the right to have the police not prosecute him on his own illegal deals. It is a silly game. A rule of thumb is that snitches claim they can do anything, which is always a lie. They rarely look you in the eye. If you have any doubts, put the shithead under surveillance. Follow him (or her). A snitch will run right to the law.

Always have a company for your operations—MM Traders, Imports of Florida, or whatever. Get a post office box and a phone service away from where you live. Never use your home phone for business. Make up good-looking business cards. Always wear good clothes, a suit or sportscoat and quality shoes. Buy a Rolex watch or a counterfeit Rolex watch. People will want to see you as a success. Drive a later model car, but not a Lincoln or Cadillac Seville. Remember you are what you think you are. Be a business executive, not a devious planner. You are in the game for money, just like Exxon.

Keep your hair short and your appearance neat and clean. One of the worst things you can do is look sloppy and thus become a target of those who enforce customs law. Many smugglers are originally targeted by law officers because of appearances and flamboyant attitudes. Do not use cash for airline tickets or for hotels. Always use credit cards. Cash should be for meals and entertainment only.

Travel first class in a business suit at peak traveling hours between 8:00 and 11:00 A.M. and 4:00 and 7:30 P.M. Businessmen always go to motels after 7:30 P.M. They rarely travel on late-night flights.

The vast majority of smugglers who get caught are drug smugglers. Rarely do you pick up the paper and read headlines about a Rolex watch smuggler or counterfeit jeans smuggler busted for his trade. Usually at worst you get a slap on the wrist if you get caught.

Let us look at the enforcers. Most police authorities have similar structures and attitudes. Customs agents all the way to local police are in the big bust business. They envision themselves as heroes busting a big coke dealer. Most don't know Jordache jeans or Rolex watches from Levis or a Timex. Their enforcement procedures are set up to bust druggers or big money movers. Smaller operators float through every day.

One customs inspector friend told me all about their use of the individual "profile" sheet. He was always looking for the big drug dealer. He wanted a promotion and knew he'd win approval if he could pop the druggers.

Airplanes are not always the best mode of travel for smugglers. This is so because all enforcement units from the local to the federal level have their own airport watch and surveillance teams. Imagine walking around airport lobbies eight to ten hours a day looking at people and trying to spot the smugglers. Boring, boring, boring. Anyone with even a little intelligence wouldn't do such a job. They can only get the obvious, so if you get caught at an airport check, you are a fool. Still, with from four to six teams of agents cruising the airport lobbies, you may just as well take a cruise ship. If air travel is necessary, get a haircut and dress conservatively in a dark or charcoal suit, wingtip shoes, and white shirt, and carry used luggage. Carry the *Wall Street Journal* and don't loiter. Treat it all as a game— but think business.

Cruise ships are an easy way to go, and more often than not are much less strict in the customs area.

We recently noted that even the French are into

smuggling, because of the new Mitterrand government. We include this news item to show how and why the good clean-cut French businessman is moving or smuggling money out of the country.

Wealthy French Smuggle Money

PARIS (AP)—Frightened by Socialist President François Mitterrand's soak-the-rich policy and his nationalization program, wealthy Frenchmen are smuggling staggering amounts of money abroad.

Sources in French financial circles say "black money" operations began to escalate late last year when nervous, foresighted investors anticipated the defeat of conservative President Valery Giscard d'Estaing and began transferring their assets to tax havens in Switzerland, Luxembourg, Liechtenstein and the Bahamas.

The customs agents' union estimates as much as $5.7 billion may have been sent out of the country illegally since Mitterrand won the presidency May 10.

The customs department reported it seized $3 million at frontier posts in August and September and said this may have been only the tip of the iceberg.

It is illegal to take more than $1,100 worth of francs out of the country, but most of the currency violation cases have far exceeded that amount.

With an eye on upper-crust smugglers, the government has increased customs controls at borders crossed by 251 million people last year. But it admits some of the heavily traveled frontiers—particularly the 142-mile border with Switzerland, a traditional money haven— cannot be guarded completely.

New tax laws have panicked many wealthy French. To fund a shorter work week, more government jobs to ease unemployment and other social programs, Mitterrand has slapped the affluent with a wealth tax, raised inheritance and business taxes and put higher taxes on yachts and other luxuries.

Twenty-one people have been charged with violating currency laws since Nov. 2 in cases that made front-page headlines. The accused include a former bank president and the president of one of the largest chains of appliance stores.

Police in the northern industrial city of Lille announced Friday that six people had been charged with illegally transferring about $3.5 million to Switzerland. Investigators said they stumbled on the operation when they searched the car of the president of a Lille public works firm during a routine check at the Swiss border. Although police claimed the smugglers had been at work for several years, they said the operation speeded up considerably in the past few weeks.

The biggest case so far involves one of the thirty-six banks the government is going to nationalize, along with two other financial institutions and five industrial groups.

Customs agents paid an unannounced visit to the Banque de Paris et des Pays-Bas, or Paribas, searched its records and filed suit

Nov. 9 charging that $32.1 million had been transferred illegally to a Swiss affiliate. Charges were filed against five of the bank's officers, including the former president Pierre Moussa, and ten clients.

It should be noted here that while the U.S. Supreme Court has heard testimony on the Drug Enforcement Administration's standardized "profile" airport smuggler's sheets, it matters little to us. Good smugglers avoid the profile completely by not looking like smugglers.

When police agents stopped Mark Royer in Miami International Airport in 1978, they did so because he fit the profile. He made the following mistakes:

- He paid cash for his tickets.
- He gave airline desk personnel a name other than his own.
- He acted nervous and uneasy.
- He kept looking behind him to see if people were watching.
- He dressed in clothes other than a business suit.
- He used an airport pay-phone.

Nick Navarro, head of Fort Lauderdale's Organized Crime Bureau, runs the most intensive airport surveillance and search unit in the country. He goes by the "profile," and many of his people are tough, demanding, and overzealous. He receives our highest award for airports to stay away from if you do decide to enter the smuggling business.

Police made over one hundred arrests last year just on this one "profile." They also seized over sixteen million dollars worth of booty. In Fort Lauderdale airport agents Ralph Capone and James Carl seem to get most of the action. Remember cops lie just like everyone else, and if you don't believe it, just see the movie *Prince of the City.*

Don't put yourself on a "my word versus your word" situation with the law. Juries almost always believe the cops, even if the cops lie as they have done in the past and will do in the future; and when you fall, it is a long drop.

Now we are going to list the toughest and the easiest airports in the U.S.A.

Toughest

Fort Lauderdale	Don't travel here.
Kennedy, New York	Customs can be tough here, but local cops are soft, and can be deceived.
Chicago—O'Hare	Seems this airport is seasonal—easy in winter, awful in summer—customs are tough.
Los Angeles	This place is a mess. Police here follow the profile sheet to a T. Customs here are just obnoxious, but can be beaten.
Miami	Airport surveillance people tough. Customs is so-so, but lines are long. Customs usually on lookout for coke-carrying Columbians and other aliens. The women inspectors are to be avoided.

Easiest

Dallas	Unless you're a fool, you can float on through.

Jacksonville, Florida	Good old southern hospitality. Just move real slow like everyone else.
Atlanta	Huge quagmire of people, planes, cars. Easy to blend in, but you must wear a suit. Sheer numbers let you smoke through.
Boston	Easiest international airport in U.S.A. It's a wonder—law enforcement people look good, easy to spot. Just keep your direction and run along.
Denver	Carry skis and go through in winter months. No problem.

It is better to use middle-sized air facilities like Palm Beach, Florida; San Jose, California; Bangor, Maine; or perhaps Westchester County, New York. All domestic lines connect to these, and some are even used for certain international flights.

The most important thing you can prepare in this business is your mind. You are the aggressor. You pick the time and the place, and the opposition is too small to be everywhere all the time. Just consider if statistics state that only 10 percent of all drug smugglers get caught, then only about .01 percent of other types of smugglers get caught. Now, those are fairly appealing odds, even if you're a novice in the gamblers' or pirates' world.

Doing the research for this book, we spoke with a variety of smugglers. One was a weapons smuggler. He never filed flight plans to the Bahamas in his own plane. He loaded his contraband guns into his small Cessna 210 turbo in diving bags. Yes, skin diving bags and false air tanks. Then he carried his booty to an island in the Bahamas where he had a connection. Bahamians have always been pirates, and any good Bahamian knows where and how to smuggle. All of history's pirates, from Henry Morgan to Jean Lafitte, used Bahamians and the 700 islands of the Bahamas to smuggle gold and silver, pieces of eight, and anything else worth money.

Well, this gunrunner never had customs problems in the Bahamas, and when he had to return to Florida, he simply gassed up and flew directly back to North Perry Airport or Fort Pierce Airport. He never went to customs and he never had problems. Why? Well, he used inconspicuous planes and always just flew into the airport and parked. Nothing but four thousand to sixty-five hundred dollars profit to unload, so if anyone did watch he saw nothing. The gunrunner usually made one trip a week and generally made a profit of between sixteen thousand and twenty-five thousand each month. During our talks, he said that he had been in the business for over four years. Now, that's good money.

Let us talk briefly about dress codes and lifestyle. There is an old saying that you dress the way you think that you are. In other words, you are in life what you believe you are. One problem the average scammer or smuggler has is that he lives his lifestyle: long hair, gold jewelry, fast cars, lots of girls, large houses. This creates problems. One must learn the art of toning down his or her lifestyle. Buy in residential neighborhoods and become family-oriented. Once neighbors accept you as a legitimate life insurance salesman, you are in like Flynn. Good neighbors are an asset that can serve to protect you rather than hurt you. Be conservative, for most American subdivisions are liberal to conservative in style.

Remember to set up a regular work routine so that people can testify that you work from 8:30 A.M. to 5:00 P.M. on a regular basis. Conduct all your liaisons with young women away from your residence. Resort motels are more charming, and desk clerks never remember people's names or faces.

Establish breakfast locations to eat almost every day at the same time. Waitresses will get to know you and will always remember you. This can be good for alibis and character references. Most of these women will take up for you if you tip well and are friendly. Such established areas or safe sites are called target areas of pocket resistance. Private establishments will almost always help good customers—remember, it is to their advantage, for good customers are hard to find. Pocket resistance areas are what we'll term "passive," and they take a great deal of cultivation to establish correctly.

When you develop this lifestyle, people will come to your aid. Attend church regularly. This is most important. There are several reasons for this. First, if you want to dance, you must pay the band. Second, in times of trouble, ministers are good to have on your team. Donate regularly to church funds and live ethically. Remember that smuggling is a business, and you are establishing both an active and a passive profile in your business.

Happiness is not a state to arrive at, but a manner of traveling.

Margaret Lee Runbeck

2. Building the Organization

THERE ARE SEVERAL THINGS TO remember when entering the smuggling business. It should be fully understood that you must start small, test the waters, and move slowly uphill. Start small, then progress, as all the big corporations of the world did. Now, luck does have a lot to do with long range successes, but "chance favors a prepared mind." Many would-be smugglers join already existing organizations. The problem arises when these organizations are not security conscious enough and become penetrated by law enforcement persons (confidential informants or snitches). Then the whole organization suffers and you receive a "conspiracy" rap for nothing. The lesson to learn here is to start your own organization and begin with just yourself. Remember the old cliche, "if you want it done right, do it yourself."

Egos become people's biggest problems. Most large-scale smugglers get caught because of their own belief that they are invincible. They begin to deal more and more in the open and want everyone to know their occupation. There is one point to emphasize here: Drug smuggling is a short-term business. One should never stay in it. Prisons are overflowing with dopers with egos too big for their own good.

Begin by first identifying the commodity or product that you wish to import or export. It does not really break U.S. law to buy refrigerators, televisions and microwave ovens. Load them on your DC-3 airplane and fly them to a clandestine airstrip in Mexico. Your Mexican connection then takes the items for cash. You have violated Mexican customs by not paying duties, but quite frankly, who cares? Many people I know of are rich today because they flew TVs and cigarettes past Mexican customs and paid no duties. It is said that a Beech-18-load of such electrical and electronics items brings a two thousand to twenty-five hundred dollar profit to you per trip. Now, that isn't bad. Make the trip one a week and you have ten thousand dollars cash a month for maybe five to six days work.

I have even heard of a man who flew cigarettes in a single engine Cherokee-6 from North Carolina to New York State. He did it twice a week, and after seven years' work is now retired and wealthy to boot. He flew alone, unloaded alone, and had again a good connection in New York.

Once you have gotten your feet wet a little and identified your product and connection wherever they may be, it is time to test all the systems. A dry run in any sort of smuggling venture is a worthwhile practice. It is good for your own ego and helps you to deal with the unexpected things that so often permeate this business.

Now you start the business of smuggling. Once you've made a few trips and you begin to feel more at ease, you may want a friend to help. Never introduce a friend to your foreign connection—now I mean *never*. Never admit a stranger to your team unless he has been thoroughly tested by polygraph by your security people. If you *fully* trust your friend, okay.

This is a good time to introduce security. Always think security. If you stay small, no big deal, but if you want to grow, you need the following:

- Electronics people (debuggers).
- Polygraph person—could double as electronics man.
- Lawyer—should be fully trusted and on a retainer.
- Several safe locations in different states.
- Legitimate business front, preferably a restaurant or other cash front.

Never grow too big too fast at your game. Move very cautiously, slowly, and remember to be satisfied with what profits you can make. Greed is evil, and it has done many people in. There is another thing to remember: behind every great fortune there is a crime.

Telephones

The phone is the twentieth century's most damning piece of equipment, and many a person is in jail today because his or her voice was recorded on a tapped phone. Police have recorded thousands of hours of phone conversations to make one case. Most smugglers eventually get lazy and don't want to go to the pay phone. Well, you'll be in jail if you get too lazy. Remember, both parties must be at pay phones—so call your contact from a pay phone and have him call your pay phone number from another pay phone. This is a simple procedure, but effective.

Cars

If you are an active smuggler, rent or lease a simple standard vehicle and store it away from home. This will be your work car. Never use a good expensive car for work. They tend to stick out, and in your business you must blend in. Your company car should, of course, be leased in your company name. Put as few possessions as possible in your own name. Remember, under the RICO Act police can seize anything with a direct connection to you.

Lawyers

Lawyers are a necessary evil in the business. They can break you financially, but they can also keep you out of jail. It is surprising that in our society, where there are millions of lawyers, there are so few *good* trial or criminal lawyers. Perhaps the reason is that a trial lawyer must be an excellent actor, and few good actors choose to go into law.

Do beware of the hotshot lawyers. Also remember a good lawyer in Miami can easily be a dud in Dallas. If you must hire an attorney, find one locally. He will know the customs, judges and behind-the-scenes procedures that are necessary for a successful conclusion to your problem.

Passports

Get a counterfeit passport now! Here's how:

1. Search vital records, tombstones, obituaries, morgues, and so on, and locate the names of people who died as babies or children. The year of birth should be approximately the same as yours. You are looking for a subject that cannot have applied for, or have been granted, a social security card.

2. From all data on the death records, go to the state records office and apply for a duplicate birth certificate.

3. Use your new birth certificate for a driver's license, a social security card, and a voter's registration, all in the alias name.

4. Later, with documents in hand, apply for a passport. No problem at all—just use it and run.

Remember you can buy phony documents out-of-country in many locations. You can fly to the Bahamas, Central America, Canada, and many Caribbean Islands with no passport at all.

If you know a printer you can rely on, he can make anything in the I.D. line for you.

You also might like to write to:

Born Again Publications
P.O. Box 344
Columbus, Ohio 43215

These people offer birth certificates by mail. These alone are good enough to use for travel to many foreign countries.

Mail Forwarding Services

Mail forwarding services are quite handy, and they operate with the blessings of the U.S. Postal Service. They allow you to have a postal address in another town, even another state. The forwarding service then sends your mail on to your private address at home or at the office.

It is a good idea to spike your mail once in a while. Run a test piece through the mail forwarding service every now and then. It is also good not to have any return address on sensitive mail as our local federal agents often snoop on first-class mail. If you check your mail every day and you see the condition of the letters looks suspicious, then use better precautions. Mail intercepts and snooping by the DEA and FBI are done poorly; your letter will bear the signs. The CIA is the only government agency with *good* flaps and seals people.

Remember, if you do not wish to receive any mail you can simply have your own rubber stamps printed so that you stamp the *unopened* letter received with the following:

- Deceased
- Moved—No Forwarding Address
- Not Deliverable as Addressed—Unable to Forward

You can order rubber stamps to fit any need that you may have.

A large portion of your profits should be put into your legitimate cash flow business for laundering purposes. Actually, you could move the money directly to offshore banks in the Bahamas or the Cayman Islands. The best way to do this is by charter jet or your own plane. Don't wire money. You also should obtain a private safety deposit box from one of the new safety deposit box companies. These are more secure than banks, much less regulated than banks, and you are a number, not a name. (Use some of the phony, or paper trip, identifications that we suggested earlier.)

It is a good time to remember that in any legitimate corporation there is only one "honcho," or chairman of the board. You must set the structure up yourself and run all small parts. Only one person must make all the important decisions. If you work alone, of course, you simplify the matter easily and efficiently.

You should not mention your side business of smuggling to anyone. Don't talk about it to your wife or girlfriends because they talk, and if the subject gets to the wrong ears, problems arise. This is not an ego trip, it is what is known as "a monetary rewards program," or MRP. While money can be the root of all evil, it also allows one to have one hell of a lot of fun. The Bible even states in the New Testament that it is easier for a camel to pass through the eye of a needle than it is for a rich man to get to heaven.

Smuggler's Business Structure

Chairman of
Board

Yourself
Electronics
Polygraph
Security
Surveillance

Lieutenant
Most Trusted Friend
Number Two Man

Operation
Personnel

Subordinates, Drivers,
Pilots, Boat, Errand
Runners

The idea is to isolate yourself more and more as you develop as a company. It is a simple structure, but effective, and it can be enlarged as you grow.

The following is an article from the *Miami Herald* about their smuggler of the week. It shows how *not* to smuggle gold.

All That Gold Leads to Siberia

Smuggler of the Week: Z. Nalgiev of the Union of Soviet Socialist Republics, was tripped up by a blatting metal detector at the Magadan Airport in Siberia and discovered to have reposed in his stomach 10 rubber packets full of gold dust. Mr. Nalgiev indignantly denied knowledge of everything and said he couldn't imagine how he happened to have 10 rubber packets full of gold dust in his stomach. He has been sentenced to seven years at hard labor.

Russia frowns on smugglers, but smuggling is part of their heritage and takes place every day in all Russian seaports.

The following is a list of products and where they can be smuggled to. These can give you food for thought.

Guns—Central America, South America, South Africa

It is not illegal in the United States to buy guns and give them away or even sell them. Make a connection and buy untraceable guns at gun shows for a lot less money and no paper work. Box them in kids' toy boxes, gift-wrap them, and stuff them into a suitcase. It helps to get a buyer, a connection to get you through customs in your host country. You'll double your money easily. Maybe even triple it.

In South Africa, if you're white, you are allowed to bring in five guns, and customs lets you get by with seven. You'll triple your money here. They love Colt .45 or 9mm automatics. Many people make two to three thousand dollars pocket money on this run.

Televisions, Refrigerators, Microwave Ovens— Central and South America and the Caribbean

This is easy. You may be breaking Mexican customs

laws, but in Mexico, as well as in 98 percent of the Caribbean and the Americas, graft or small payoffs known as *mordida* get you through. Get a good connection and you can double or triple your money. In today's economy you can make a deal with someone. Latins are peddlers at heart, so any legitimate businessman in Latin America can get you started. They all know someone.

Watches: Rolex, Patek Phillip, Cartier, and Others—United States and Europe

There are two ways to play this game: buy from Europe and import originals, or, even easier, make a New York or Miami connection and buy fakes. These fakes are excellent. Sell them to friends or anyone else. They are exact copies, and you can buy the Cartiers for seventy-five dollars, Rolex from two hundred to three hundred dollars. Big status symbol items. Many people even run off to places like Italy and sell them as originals to Italians or tourists. You could easily develop a three thousand to five thousand dollar a month business here. This would be even part-time money.

Cigarettes—United States or Anywhere

Buy in North Carolina and drive these goodies anywhere. Sell initially to friends. You'll find millions of people hooked on this habit. Profit comes from cigarettes because taxes differ in each state. The North Carolina state tax is much lower than most. You won't double your money, but a handsome profit exists here once you get a bulk buyer.

There are numerous other goodies to import or export. Emeralds from Colombia (every bimbo there sells them, but take a gemology class before you go), furs from Canada—and go to Hong Kong, where you can

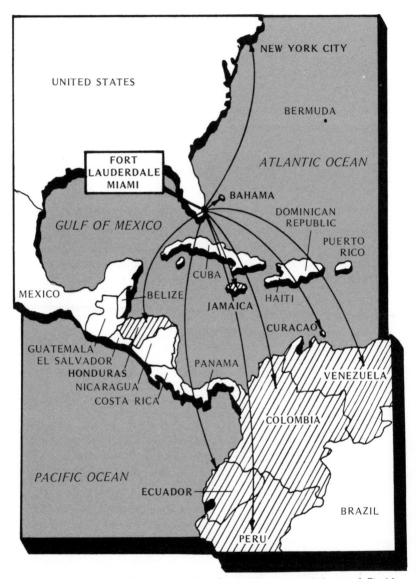

Map showing some of the destinations for handguns smuggled out of Florida.

There's plenty of money to be made from selling exact copies of famous brand name watches (although the original companies frown on it mightily). Sell them as fakes, or try to pass them off as originals. The watches shown are all counterfeit.

buy or sell anything. Places to check out for starting into the business:

Colombia

Bogota Hilton or Tecandama Hotels—many emeralds here.
Cartagena—any of the beach hotels. But be careful, the military uses these.
Santa Marta—smuggler's heaven. Any beach hotel.
Barranquilla—intercontinental.

Guatemala

Camino Real—go to Zone One Market Place. Easy to make contacts. Also, lots of Americans go to the Ritz Hotel Bar, in Zone One. Fiesta Hotel Casino in Zone Ten, just off the Reforma Boulevard, is good.

El Salvador

They need everything—go stay at the Camino Real or Hilton. Remember, keep away from reporters.

Belize

Hopeless place, but a port of call for lots of smugglers. Try Belize City or Belmopan.

Mexico

Just about anywhere here because they smuggle everything in and out.

Bahamas

Good place for smuggling Haitians into the United States. Bimini is good; just hang around the airport. Likely you'll get propositioned. Grand Bahama Island, Mores Island, Sandy Point, Cat Key, and

Great Harbour, all smuggler's heavens.
They play for keeps here. Rent a Cessna 150, hop
over and scavenge these islands. Lots of people
doing business here, but loaded with snitches and
doublecrossers. Be careful.

Europe (France)

Marseille—check all port or coast areas. Great for big
timers.

Haiti

Stay at the El Rancho or downtown at the Olondorf
Hotel or Holiday Inn. Lots of good contacts; even
Duvalier's brother-in-law has been arrested for
smuggling. Great place to visit, and any Haitian who
smells profits is willing to help. Lots of gold smuggled through both Cap Haitien and Port-au-Prince.
In Cap Haitien stay at the Mt. Joli. All the people
up on the North Coast are pirate smugglers.

Well, we've tried to give you some food for thought
here.

Women

One of the interesting things about smuggling is all
the women you meet. The young ones, eighteen to
twenty-eight, love the pirate flare and they have great
fantasies of being in some great adventure. You'll
receive all the sex imaginable, with regularity and
variety.

While staying at the Princess in Freeport, a friend of
mine told a young Canadian girl he was a smuggler. She
(beautiful) had heard so much about smuggling in the
Bahamas, she flew from Montreal to check it out. When

she met Willie (not his name), she balled his brains out and wanted to hear more stories. Hell, he made them up. Each time she'd get hotter and hotter, the stories got hotter and more outlandish, and her orgasms erupted the more she heard.

Willie laughed about this to me, and said the Canadian girl even had her girlfriend join in a *ménage à trois* triangle so she could hear the stories. It is crazy, but gold and money attract young women, and they're almost at your command.

When I asked Willie how it ended, he said, "Shit, I couldn't make up any more stories." He was exhausted. The Canadian girls went home to their drab life with stories of pirates, sex in the surf, tropical paradises, and even new fantasies. This is what makes the world interesting.

You must realize the vast majority of people in the world are bored stiff. Same routine—no flare—sex after 10:00 P.M. if one isn't too tired—eat at McDonald's—clothes to wash. People don't even take care of themselves; just look at all the fat, out-of-shape specimens we see every day. Their world is soap operas—TV and little else. So when they meet you, a pirate, their knees become weak, and you are off to a world of pleasure.

History is an account,
mostly false,
of events,
mostly unimportant,
which are brought about by rulers,
mostly knaves,
and soldiers,
mostly fools.

Ambrose Bierce

3. Drug Smuggling

WE HAVE STAYED AWAY FROM THE drug business on purpose until now. We do not condone this enterprise, but it must be discussed because it is the largest smuggling business in the world. Drugs are dirty products which can bring great harm. Unfortunately, people associate smugglers with drugs, as if all smugglers were dope transporters, and this just is not the case. However, drugs have created the channels and boundaries of most smuggling routes.

There is enormous profit in drugs, and this tends to corrupt the law enforcement community and smugglers alike. It is a fact that many police have their own drug operations, and we have been told that some prominent business people buy drugs for personal use from police connections. Drugs are a violence-oriented product, and we recommend other products which are not linked to violence.

Enough on that, so on we'll go into the constantly churning world of drug traffickers and pushers.

By smuggling televisions, coffee, cigarettes, Cartier watches, and other product commodities you are beating the system and the tax structure. Uncle Sam totally pisses away our money anyway, so beat him at his own game. Become part of the subterranean economy. When you get into drugs you stand a chance of hurting others either through the intake of your product or by a problem at sea or in the air. We in Florida read every day of those who wash up dead on Florida beaches as a result of storms or mechanical failure. Countless others are never heard from again. The very nature of the drug trade and its association with huge profits dictates violence and often violates character.

If you become a drug smuggler, stay small. Remember the law wants the big guns like "The Company," or "The Sunburn Corporation of Key West," or the famous yet absurd "Black Tuna Gang." There are many more one can name, like the Burnstein Group or the De Lisi gang.

There is a lesson to be learned here, as all these groups are dead, in jail, or on the run, being hunted by bondsmen and federals alike. The lesson is: *drugs are a short term business,* unless you stay small and can be satisfied with two hundred- to three hundred-pound marijuana runs to the Bahamas. Multiton loads are too easily popped. Their sheer size makes clandestinity tough. The big boys will run anything from a DC-8 down to a DC-3 and they are very successful.

Sources

The main sources of supply lie in Colombia, Mexico and Jamaica. This is becoming less true today, as more and more homegrown is cultivated in the U.S.A. This should be an avenue to explore. Lots of dope is grown on federal land, so you have no need to run out and buy a farm.

To make connections, go to any coastal cities in these countries, and you'll be approached. Never take money of any quantity with you. Dope buyers almost always buy on credit. Yes, for sure—they have insurance in case they lose a load—the whole corporate structure. All multiton loads are credit buys, so all the huge busts you read about have been insured, and these new replacement loads have already hit the street. You can rest assured the product got through and the mules transporting the busted load went to jail.

We suggest the Bahamas as the place to break into the business; the Turks and Caicos Islands, and even the island of La Tortue, off Haiti, are good. You can fly a Cessna 172 or use a twenty-foot or twenty-five-foot sport fishing boat. Cruise over to any of these islands and start inquiring. Buy 150 pounds. Hell, every Bahamian is a doper. They comb the beaches every day to get the dope, dry it, and hide it everywhere until American scavengers come asking for it. Many people buy it, put it in small lots into diving tanks with false tops, diving bags, or even stuff it into life vests. You'll pay around one hundred dollars a pound in the Bahamas, sometimes eighty dollars and sometimes one hundred twenty-five dollars.

This is clean and simple, you working alone as buyer-transporter, off loader and seller. On a 150 pound load, you'll triple your investment. I've heard of people making two to three trips a day from Miami to Freeport and back. No problem. Once you get started you'll earn from thirty thousand to fifty thousand dollars a month profit on small trips. Risk is small because cops leave the small planes alone unless they are tipped off. Boats are easy too. We've heard of one multiton king who went from DC-6's and fifteen-thousand-pound loads to various small planes, all single engine. A big plane takes his goods to the lower Bahamas, and some ten small planes move it to Florida or Texas.

Islands to get your feet wet:
- Grand Bahama Island

This Bimini dock has felt the feet of numerous Haitians, Colombians, and others who have been smuggled from Bimini's South Island.

Whether you want to buy or sell smuggled drugs, making the right contacts is important. Certain establishments are noted as being "the" places for meeting the right people, as are these two in Bimini.

- Mores Island
- Abaco
- Bimini
- Andros (all the dopers use it)
- Cat Cay
- Great Inaqua.

These are well known, but all the islands are loaded, from Great Harbour to Haiti's La Tortue. Peak traffic times are best to fly, but hell, smugglers are successful from daylight on through night hours. Fly home and to the Bahamas at an altitude no higher than five hundred feet. Actually as high as fifteen hundred feet is okay in a small single-engine plane. Don't file a flight plan anywhere.

We also suggest that south Texas is a smuggler's heaven, as is southern New Mexico from Las Cruces on to Tucson, Nogales, Yuma, and into California. Small plane heaven—many people are making money here on the borders.

In El Paso DEA has their big computer center for intelligence, but this is of no consequence. They have radar and other goodies. Close to 96 percent of all drug flights in south Texas on to southern Arizona are successful; only about 91 percent are successful in Florida. There is an expression that holds true for the drug business: "big balls, big bucks." Most dopers are not real fearful people. The government can have its George Bush Task Force, but it is of little value because the "product" *will* get through.

The problem is, many people in smuggling drugs love war between cops and feds—this is a game, a challenge. Hell, many pilots know they're being watched leaving Florida, and they give the middle finger sign to the watching agents. Now that's part crazy. It would make no difference if there were a thousand federal agents and the whole Marine Corps in Florida. The profits are great, so the product will get through, period. There is no disputing it. Our government is wasting time and a horrendous amount of money fighting an absolutely impossible problem. Plainly and simply, they are kidding George Bush and themselves.

Cocaine oftentimes follows the same routes as does marijuana. It is a problem of enormous magnitude.

If you somehow dig this business, got to Colombia. In Bogota you can make connection in the park across from the Tecandama Hotel. Buy small lots and transport it on you all the way back. Don't fly from Colombia to the United States. Fly from Colombia to Guatemala or Panama, then to the Bahamas. Preclear customs in Nassau and you're in. Always dress for the occasion. Dress is very important.

If you come from Colombia direct, wear a dark, conservative suit. Wingtip shoes are also advisable. Your hair should be short and neat. Have business cards printed showing that you are a lawyer. You'll whistle through.

. . . If you won't plow in the cold you won't eat in the Harvest.

Proverbs 20.4

4. The Bounties of Countries

BOLIVIA IS A DUMPY PLACE, A LAND-locked country with few resources other than tin for legal export. Its economy is awful, so anyone with sense becomes a smuggler. What Bolivia does have is a perfect climate for coca plants. If you want to make connections, Bolivia is the place. The cocaine trade is flourishing here. Fly to La Paz, change planes, and fly to Santa Cruz. By car or plane, travel to the town of Zinahote or Cochabamba in the Chapare Region.

Officials say the production of cocaine has never been so good. The Bolivian peasants have never had it so good. It is, they say, "completely out of control." The past military regimes were all linked to the cocaine trade, but on October 10, 1982, Hernan Siles Zuazo, age sixty-nine, took control of a huge mess. There is no clear-cut policy on coca, so the trade continues. Zinahote is clearly the center of business. One American, Harold Marlin of Cochabamba, stated that he'd been offered up to five kilos right in the Zinahote central market. Zinahote is about a three-and-a-half hour drive from Cochabamba.

Winston Estremadoiro, head of a joint U.S./Bolivian alternative crops program, has stated that the trafficking of cocaine is now out in the central markets of the

41

region. Many Americans and Western Europeans travel here for good prices and open connections. The coca leaf production this year was over thirty-five thousand metric tons in the Chapare Region alone. The Yungas Region will have a harvest of over ten thousand metric tons.

One gram of clean cocaine refined from coca leaves that sells for about four dollars in Zinahote will bring about two hundred fifty dollars on the streets of any major U.S. city.

One ton of coca leaves will yield about three kilos of cocaine. Art Medina, DEA's top man in Bolivia, says that many Bolivian traffickers can handle up to one thousand kilos at a time.

One must remember that danger is a companion to easy money. Peasants carry rifles and bandits hunt for easy prey. Some 70 percent of all Bolivians chew the coca leaf; it is as much a part of Bolivia's culture as fried chicken is to the culture of the United States.

What Zinahote is to cocaine, Santa Cruz and Trinidad are to the parrot and wild bird trade. Neighbor Brazil does not allow the export of wild tropical birds, but Bolivia does. What happens is that Bolivian bird catchers cross into Brazil, trap their prey, and return with their catch to Bolivia. Tropical birds are inexpensive here. In Santa Cruz you can buy a macaw for thirty dollars; in Miami they go for up to two thousand dollars apiece. You can get a blue-fronted Amazon parrot for about ten dollars in Santa Cruz; in Miami they sell for over four hundred dollars apiece. All the town markets sell birds. Hook up with a catcher, then connect with big bird importers like Pet Farms of Miami, and you're in business.

It may be worth your investment to look into this country as a potential area of operation. Graft is a way

Certain types of smugglers' booty may "talk." The blue-fronted Amazon parrot shown above is a high-ticket, though fairly fragile, bit of merchandise.

of life here. Remember, all the Nazi high command fled here after the fall of Germany, so graft has *always* been a way of life here.

Brazil

Cocaine is a new way of life for the upper Amazon. This area is like the old West, and anything can be bought here. Check out the towns of Esperonca for birds. They are shipped across the river to Colombia for export.

Gunrunning is big all along the Amazon, and firearms bring a pretty price.

Fly from Bogota to Leticia, Colombia. An American runs the town. Actually, he's Creek I guess. The connections will be easy to make.

Manaus is looking for industrial goods and numerous other products from the U.S.A. which can be carefully brought in.

Colombia

Just about everything imaginable comes in and out of Colombia. Marijuana and coffee are the main export, but cocaine and wild birds are big too.

Fly to Bogota. The main cocaine business is done in Medellin. The marijuana business is centered in Santa Marta and Rio Hacha. Check out Santa Marta and Barranquilla first, then travel to the town of Maicoa on the Venezuela border on the Guajira, for anything you want is available in Maicoa. Wild birds and everything else flourish here. On the coast of the Guajira from Santa Marta to Puerto Estrella, there are literally hundreds of clandestine air fields and small ports for smuggling. Most smugglers get started by simply going there to begin the search for a foreign connection. San Marcos used to be the hottest dope area in Colombia at one time.

The people-smuggling business is big in Colombia. With drugs the primary product for this country and coffee second, people-smuggling is in a solid third place. People-smugglers can be dangerous, but they run their business very effectively and very profitably.

They use two main routes. One is overland through Mexico, a week long trip. The other is by air to the Bahamas, primarily to Bimini and Nassau. From the Bahamas the people are flown by small private planes or taken by fast speedboats to Florida. Colombians also use Port-au-Prince, Haiti as a staging area before the people are moved north to the Bahamas. People-smugglers arrange everything from passports to hotel reservations. They are paid handsomely for their work, and their success rate is very high.

The best counterfeiting of documents in all Latin America is done in Colombia. It is very easy to purchase fake driver's licenses, phony passports, or almost anything else there. A phony Colombian passport would be good to have in case you were ever in need of a fast escape.

There are literally dozens of big Colombian people-smuggling groups in existence today. We suggest looking into making contact with the people on Bimini. Check the Buccaneer Hotel on South Island near the Cut or the Caruso Restaurant in Bogota. This is a staging area, and maybe if you're a pilot or boat enthusiast you'll profit. The standard price per head per trip is between six hundred and one thousand U.S. dollars.

The worst punishment one gets for smuggling aliens is about a year in jail. The getting-caught rate for alien traffickers is about .5 percent, and the prosecution rate is very low.

Patrick Bell, a Miami resident recently convicted of alien smuggling, told the press that it is an easy business to enter into. He claims his profits exceeded sixty thousand dollars for less than eighteen months work. Bell stated that on a trip from Bimini or other islands in the chain, smugglers should carry no money. Always have a friend or associate transport the money back from the islands. This stops your passengers' temptation to dump you over the side. Also, if you are caught, the feds will not be able to take your hard-earned money and use it as evidence against you. Remember to give baseball caps to your passengers and look as realistic as possible. Again, remember you picked up your passengers at sea off a wrecked boat, a good excuse in the Florida seas.

We have seen over two hundred Colombians waiting to be transported one afternoon at the Buccaneer Hotel, the docks crammed with boats waiting to transport the cargo. The opportunity is there; you have to grab it.

Always drop aliens off at a dock and make sure they have a phone nearby. Most of these people have relatives in the Florida area and can vanish quickly into the south Florida multiculture scene.

By the way, Patrick Bell received a suspended sentence upon his guilty plea and simply walked off free.

Guns are another hot item in Colombia. Two major guerrilla groups operate here, the M-19 and FARC (Armed Revolutionary Forces of Colombia). The main operational area is in Caqueta State. The town of Florencia is the best place to get started. Jaime Perez, a dope smuggler, used to run marijuana to the United States, then pick up guns in Cuba and run them to M-19 back in Colombia. He made money at both ends of the Caribbean. He loved to drop off his weapons near the Colombian town of Pizarro. He even sailed through the Panama Canal loaded with guns bound for Pizarro or Pichima.

Jaime Perez got arrested in Mexico, but lo and behold, they let him go.

Colombia is a great place to smuggle emeralds from. Some 90 percent of the world's emeralds come from Colombia. One can drive to the emerald mines from Bogota. It is advisable to take a gemology class so you can tell quality.

Many a drug smuggler has good emerald collections. A handsome profit can be made, but it is a very dangerous business. If you check into the Tecandama or Hilton hotels people will find you.

The Bahamas

Well, we must say, as history has always proven, the 700 islands of the Bahamas are the drop-off point for all the pirates of the Caribbean. Since the days of the famous Henry Morgan and Jean Lafitte, Blackbeard and all the others, the Bahamas reign as king of all the black markets. With isolated coves, numerous islands, and balmy weather, the Bahamas are ideal for year-round smuggling opportunities.

The Bahamas are our pick for a place to begin and get one's feet wet in black market trades.

People from as far away as Bangladesh travel here to gain illegal entry into the United States. Because of the islands' proximity to the United States, access is quite easy. Novices begin smuggling careers here; all that is needed is a boat or small plane. If you fly over such places as Bimini, Grand Bahama Island, Andros, and the Exumas, you can spot wrecked planes, pieces of boats, all the results of failures that occurred months before. Many have lost their lives here, and many more will in the days, months and years ahead.

Unusual talk of all kinds goes on at the Pirate's Den Bar in Bimini.

This Bimini dock has felt the feet of numerous Haitians, Colombians,

Basically, all Bahamians have smugglers' blood in them; it is simply part of Bahamian culture and their life on the sea.

Begin by exploring Bimini. It is close to the United States, and Chalk Airlines has daily flights to the only town, Alice Town. Move freely to the Anchor or the Big Game Club. Explore Hemmingway's Bar and drift down to the docks to see the big fast Scarab and Cigarette Racing boats waiting for a load. Then go south to South Island and witness the wrecked planes along its airport runway. View the bullet holes in damaged B-26 bombers, crashed Aero Commanders, and wrecked DC-4's. Watch the natives of Bimini and see their gold Rolex watches and no visible means of support.

The smuggler's prize being carried on this ill-fated airplane never reached its destination.

This has been smuggler's heaven for years. When it is not illegal whiskey, it is illegal aliens or drugs. This is the center of quick activity and fast money. In the evening, eat at the Red Lion, then move down Alice Town's main street to Brown's Bar. You'll soon get the flavor of island life.

If you want to smuggle people to Florida from Bimini, the price is $1,000 a head. You can easily make two trips a day in a Cessna 172 and earn up to $8,000 a day. A good Bimini contact helps. Check with the bar across from the Big Game Club for help. Spend a week here and all sorts of opportunity will present itself; don't be shy, just cautious.

South Island is run mainly by Colombian merchants. It is kind of a closed society here.

Moving southeast, you come to the largest Bahamian Island, Andros. This is pirate's heaven. The airstrips at North Andros, Andros Town, Andros Central, Congo Town and most others are constantly being used by smugglers. The island is the major stash area for large marijuana hauls, and it is also under constant aerial surveillance by the George Bush Blockade stoppers based at Homestead Airbase. The blockade is more a nuisance than an effective deterrent to today's pirates. Under the Bush Blockade Section of this handbook we'll see how this works and operates. There will be twelve new blockades in effect in the coming months.

Northeast of Andros are the Berry Islands. These have been the home of pirates for centuries. Stories still abound that pirates' treasures are buried here in the ocean caves. Illegal alien smuggling is big here, and few police operate in the Berries, so pretty much anything goes here. Many small one-man dope smugglers stop at Great Harbour and the other towns to buy bales from natives. The price is about one hundred dollars a pound, and even the ministers put their stashes on the block.

Andros is also a major center for illegal alien operations and even tropical birds.

Nassau, the major city in the Bahamas, is, of course, the major funneling point for illegal aliens, drugs, and all other smuggling operations. All the biggest have made this a part-time home. Robert Vesco, the Boyd Brothers, all the Black Tunas have lived and operated from this little piece of ground. Some two hundred banks and trust companies dot the main business district on Bay Street.

Nassau is now the main funneling center for our huge cash underground economy. Banking secrecy laws protect the investors, but recently the Internal Revenue Service has begun some tricky undercover operations aimed at Nassau money houses. So, smugglers beware, Big Brother wants your cash. The smuggling of cash to the Bahamian banking houses also yields big bucks, but it requires good connections. You can develop these in Nassau if you wish to devote the time and effort.

South of Nassau lies the Exuma Chain. Many of these little islands, like Norman's Key, are owned by interesting people. They are private, guarded by armed guards, and have nice airstrips. Paradise lost. Joe Lehder, a German Colombian, age twenty-eight, owned Norman's Key. New asking price is over two million dollars. There are others like Big Darby and Little Darby, all the way to Great Exuma. Police investigations have lead directly to the footsteps of Bahamian government officials.

South Caicos and Matthew Town, Great Inagua are the two leading smuggling refueling points in the Caribbean. Many planes, loaded, have stopped here for days at a time waiting for parts and an entry point into

Florida. Stay several days at either location. Little inns are available at both, and your eyes will be opened wide. It costs a standard five thousand dollars to refuel a loaded plane at both places. You can stay at Ford's Inagua Inn for about fifteen dollars a night, or at Main House for about thirty-five dollars a night.

Duncan Town, on Ragged Island in the Jumento Cays, is another doper's delight. Some smugglers store fuel here. Otherwise, none is available. There is no place to spend the night in town, but don't let that disturb you, because secluded beaches are plentiful, and during the fall dope harvesting season inexpensive bales are for sale from all the local merchants—just ask them.

Mayaguana Island is another pirate's hangout. Be careful here, for some antiHaitian and antiCuban groups train on the island from time to time, and interference in this field almost always has fatal results. If you get started in the business, Mayaguana is a good staging island and has all sorts of isolated coves and inlets. The arrival of unfamiliar private aircraft can cause quite a stir here.

Don't use Cay Sal, for it is private, and scammers already own and dominate this little jewel.

There are numerous other good islands in the Bahamas to search for black market goods, including Deadman's Cay, Cape Santa Maria, Hard Bargain, Long Island and Sandy Point. In the Abacos see Gorda Cay, Sandy Point, Scotland Cay, Treasure Cay and others. The Abacos offer many opportunities. Buy the *Pilot's Bahamian Guide* and get moving.

Grand Bahama Island is probably the second leading black market stash center in the Bahamas. Check into West End. Here is where practically all illegal aliens in the Bahamas leave from. The Jack Tarr Hotel is a comfortable place to stay, and all local natives will help you for a price. Further down is Freeport. Natives will help you here, too, but the one major caution is that this is rip-off territory. Several people have stopped breathing here because some dumb native decided to make fast money. The business is not for the squeamish. Many a plane has landed on the deserted road networks of the eastern Grand Bahama Island area, only to be trapped by natives. Shootouts, crashes, and other tragedies reminiscent of the Old West are a frequent scene on Grand Bahama.

Grand Turk—Turks/Caicos

This is yet another center for contraband trades, but don't arrive here unless you have good connections. The natives aren't too friendly, and as I know, the locals may decide they want your aircraft. Best advice is don't trust the locals.

Haiti

Well, to some this is the greatest black market heaven in the Caribbean. Port-au-Prince is dirty and poverty stricken, but boy, does money buy friendship and secrecy. Heck, even Baby Doc Duvalier's brother-in-law was rumored to be a doper. Port-au-Prince used to be a major dope refueling point and transshipment center for years. All good pirates roamed the town from Petion-Ville to Carrefour and on to La Conave.

The best center of black market trade is now Cap Haitien on the north coast. Here the Mt. Joli Hotel and others can give you restful nights. The airport has been a major refueling point for the Black Tuna Gang, the Brady Bunch, the Company, the Boyd Brothers, and many more. It used to be a flat $15,000 fee no matter the plane, but now prices are varying. Off Cap Haitien lies the Island of La Tortue, which today is a major ship refueling point.

Haiti also is a cocaine transshipment point for many of the better Cuban and Colombian drug kings. Haiti has always been a pirate's island, but Haitian craftwork and paintings offer a great resource for legitimate export businesses.

Haiti's prison, Ft. Dimanche, may be the worst one in all the Western world, so please connect yourself well on this island.

Haiti offers real opportunity for good legitimate business, so check out the low labor resources. The northwestern Haitian Coast is the main people-smuggling area, and any coastal town will help.

Jamaica

A great place to visit, and also a pirate's delight. Remember, the famous pirate Henry Morgan was the British governor here for many years. Ah, how tradition stays alive. There is only one product worth anything here, and that is dope by the bale. Negril on the west coast of the island is the center of trade. The inland mountain ranges and the Captio Church produce the Ganja, man. This island is under pressure from the Uncle to stop the flow, but more and more is ready for shipment. Ganja is Jamaica's leading export product.

Aruba/Bonaire/Curacao

Due to their proximity to Colombia's Gujira Peninsula, you can speculate what the main use of these islands is. Staging for jumps to Colombia and tourism are the mainline industries. The Dutch West Indies is also a great one for coffee smuggling and phony corporations that act as holding companies, usually for phony Panamanian corporations. On the illegal phony paper trail of scammers, the beautiful Dutch West Indies rates high on the scale. Planes, boats, and phony companies are all registered here. The illustrious Black Tuna Gang had houses on Aruba, and some of its members had boats docked here as well. This is a good area for contacts and a great place to mingle. Customs officers here are very intense, but mostly on the take. Our DEA and Customs love to play around down here, but they are usually easy to spot by their mannerisms.

This is where the great Cuban coffee rip-off was planned and developed—the one where Cuba bought coffee, some eight million dollars worth, from a phony Curacao company. It was never delivered, and the people who set up the rip-off all collected their money from Canadian banks. Cuba was left high and dry and the banks were out millions. It was a long and involved scam that worked well.

Belize

This is the growing new contraband center of the Caribbean. It is, of course, English-speaking. It is dirty and hot, and Guatemala has always claimed it as their very own. Even Belize's great Prime Minister Price has been accused of allowing drug planes to refuel—for a fee, of course. Belize is jungle and is relatively close to the United States. Dope harvested in Belize near Orange Walk and portions of the southern Mexican Yucatan Peninsula are shipped from Belize. By plane, the flight to any southern state, like Alabama, Mississippi, Louisiana, or Texas, is quick and simple. There are hundreds of entry points and numerous dead areas in our air defense radar network. Even flights to the western Florida areas are numerous. One known group was making two trips a day into Florida from Belize alone.

No one has been caught yet, but two people did die in the crash of their Aero Commander trying to pick up a load near Orange Walk. Americans run the show here, and it is a black country. Travel to Bebmopan, Belize City or Orange Walk. Contacts are easy to make, and don't be shy.

There is a growing wild bird trade as well. The much sought-after double yellow nape parrot, caught in neighboring Guatemala, is transported here for shipment to bird buyers. Export papers are easy to buy in this part of the world.

Very few export items from Belize have ever been stopped or confiscated. Numerous airfields and paved roads dot the area. This is a good place to explore because Belize has no army. The British troops here are consumers, and the jungle of Belize is neutral.

There is now a growing underground railroad of aliens that will pay up to one thousand dollars a head to get to America. One man with a Piper Navaho aircraft makes several trips a month to Belize just to pick up his aliens. He stated his monthly income as over twelve thousand dollars just from a couple of flights. There appears to be a great deal of room to grow here.

Because of the terrorist wars in Guatemala, El Salvador, and now Honduras, more and more illegals are making their way to Belize to wait to be shipped to America.

Guatemala/El Salvador/Mexico

Our opinion is that, due to guerrilla problems in all these countries, huge problems exist. The graft here is so huge it bowls you right over. The other problem is that these folks like to kill, and always have liked it.

Two Americans caught in Guatemala for illegally catching yellow nape parrots were dumped on by the

Guatemala government with the obvious help of the U.S. government. While Sam Campbell and Earl Smith broke no law whatever, they've been accused of everything. Campbell had to be smuggled out of Guatemala to Mexico and Smith ran to the U.S. embassy for help, only to be turned over to Guatemalan police by U.S. consular staff leaders.

The court system in these countries is pathetic, corrupt as hell, and virtually no competent lawyers exist at all. Just bring bricks and forget lawyers. Even U.S. Customs officer Ira Finnessy and wildlife officer Piston pushed to keep these two Americans in Guatemala's famed Secundo Querpa Prison. Not a nice place to visit. Thanks to one south Florida expert on Central American prisons, both Smith and Campbell got out, but it took time and pain and money to pull it off. The problems with Mexico are the same.

Many of Guatemala's wild birds are smuggled here for export to big buyers in the United States. All kinds of illegal drugs flourish, and smuggling gold coins to the United States has become big business now that it is illegal to take gold out of Mexico. Remember, the United States loves the gold, and it is not against the law to import it, but according to Mexico it is smuggling.

Oaxaca, Mexico, is a main export center for illegal drugs, as are Culiacan and Durango. Many Americans have been killed in the Culiacan region because large drug smugglers employ their own armies, police are all corrupt here, and the doublecross system is standard operating procedure.

Illegal aliens by the hundreds of thousands wait for transport to the United States. "Coyotes," U.S. smugglers that bring in Mexicans, can be brutal, and it is a tight community to break into. The whole 3,000-mile southern border with Mexico is an open, fair market, but dangerous.

In El Salvador the wild bird business and illegal gun trade is tops, if the Salvadorian guerrillas don't get you first.

The best opportunity of this region is helping Americans and wealthy Mexicans to smuggle gold coins and jewelry to America. Guadalajara is the center of this trade, due to its large American population. Monterrey is the second largest center, but Mexico City is catching up.

Our evaluation of Mexico is that it is a time bomb waiting to explode. Disease, poverty, and overpopulation will all wreak havoc upon Mexico.

Europe

This is the region to check for smuggling Bibles. Many churches in the United States have Bible smuggling programs. These are actual missionary ministries that work out of three main countries: West Germany, Austria and Switzerland. They employ all the same tricks that drug smugglers in the Caribbean use these days:

- False compartments in a vehicle, generally false areas in gas tanks that hold up to one hundred small Bibles;
- Other hidden areas in car or truck frames;
- Illegal flights into Eastern Europe to drop off Bibles; and
- Stash houses, clandestine operations, safe houses and factories to build transporting vehicles.

Bible smuggling is business in the missionary field. These operations are funded by Catholic, Baptist, Methodist, and virtually all other congregations. Your best place to start could be any one of the large Baptist

churches in Dallas, Atlanta or Miami. Check out the big
Baptist church in Perrine, Florida, south of Miami, or
even the large ones in Fort Lauderdale, Florida. This
smuggling is an important, worthwhile mission, and it
is not without danger. We could name names about
this, but won't, because it could only interfere with
these good works.

The churches actually fund whole factories to build
the transporting vehicles. They also fund the operators
of the scheme, all with church money. Pretty nifty
trick.

These operations are centered in Munich, Hamburg,
and two or three smaller towns on the Czechoslovakian
and East German borders.

In Switzerland, Zurich is one main area for Biblical
operations, and in Austria the center is Vienna.

It is best to get into this missionary field through
churches in the United States, for mostly nationals of
the country run these operations, while some manage-
ment and all the money comes from U.S. churches
through missionary funds.

Switzerland is the home of some fine watches.
Rolex is a fine name in gold watches. You can buy them
for less than half their U.S. value in the Swiss market
place. A gold Rolex sells for about eighty-five hundred
dollars in the United States, and they can be bought for
as low as thirty-six hundred dollars in some open Swiss
markets. If you have a jewelry connection in the United
States, smuggle two or three in and you'll be able to
sell them for about six thousand dollars to jewelers.
With only three watches, you'll make over seventy-two
thousand dollars on a single trip, less about two thousand dollars in expenses. Not bad. They are small, easy
to hide, and you'll slip right into the United States. Now
don't, for land's sake, declare them.

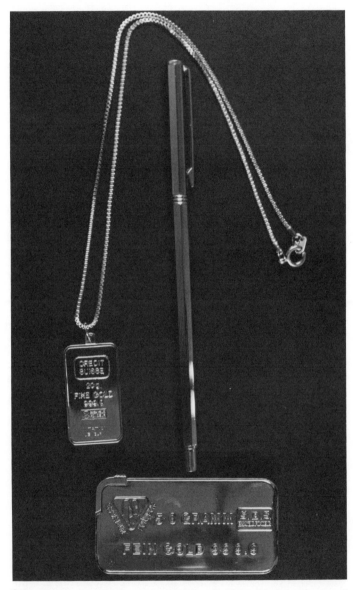

Gold always goes a long way in providing the best things in life even if it's counterfeit like the gold shown above.

You can buy all sorts of other watches and fine crafts here as well.

West Africa

In reality, Ghana, Nigeria and the others are real dumps. I've been all through the area and run into Americans even up the Congo River. There is a hell of a black market here on currency exchanges. All the West African currencies are worthless, but oh, do they want dollars.

Ivory is a smuggler's product here, but not much else is worth anything except diamonds. In Accra, Ghana, stay at the Continental Hotel near the airport. I just sat around for a week and had diamond dealers, ivory dealers, and black market traders all begging to do business. The main African marketplace in Accra is swarming with fast-dollar people, so keep a careful eye open.

Lagos, Nigeria, is so corrupt that it will cost you money to arrive and about one hundred thirty dollars just to leave the dump. There may be opportunities here, but our advice is to forget this place, for it is absolutely awful, an unfriendly, disease-ridden area where the fly and mosquito are the national birds. The Federal Place Hotel (New Section) and the Elko Holiday Inn are the only places to stay in town. Bring plenty of money; it costs big bucks here.

South Africa is a good place for guns. It is legal to bring in up to seven at a time. You won't make much, but it could be enough for a free vacation. If you enjoy mercenary zest, hang around Johannesburg and Cape Town. Many connections can be made here which may carry you to other things.

Far East

Start in Bangkok and then fly to Chianmai, Thailand. Go by car to Chiang Rai and to Mai Sai. Here, near Ban Houei Sai, is the home of the large opium lords Chung Sa, Lo Sing Hau, Chu Chia Chu, and others. Anything goes, and huge private armies control all jade and opium markets, but it is such a fascinating area that every good smuggler should see it as one.

Jade has good possibilities here, as do rubies. Your costs will be great to reach this point, and numerous obstacles could deter you.

In Hong Kong, phony Rolex and Cartier watches are great to buy for about fifteen dollars apiece. They are identical in all markings with the real Rolex and sell in America for up to six hundred fifty dollars apiece. That is a good profit.

Both Hong Kong and Taipei are centers for copies. Jordache jeans, Rolex watches, and Dior shirts are all counterfeited in these two areas. One can make a handsome profit in the counterfeit jewelry and label clothing business. Sometimes the counterfeits are in greater demand than the real thing. More than half of all Rolex and Cartier watches sold in America are fakes. In South America about two-thirds of all big-name watches and clothes are fakes. Even the sexy Porsche Design sunglasses are imitations in Hong Kong. They are made in Hong Kong and Taipei, and the marketplace becomes America. All the world's fake clocks and clothes originate here. This is the land of copies, and you can do very well by working this market. Many people make good money just selling fake Rolex, Cartier and Piaget watches. The fake or copies business has unlimited market potential anywhere in the world, but you must go to the source and invest for your future.

Well, we have given you food for thought on where and how to get started. Be careful, and remember, don't be shy, because big balls mean big bucks. Don't get stuck at boring desk jobs again! Reach out for adventure, travel and excitement.

Countries where fake Rolex watches, Cartiers, Porsche design sunglasses, fake polo shirts and Jordache jeans may be smuggled for huge profits:

United States	Ireland
Canada	West Germany
Mexico	Soviet Union
Guatemala	Poland
Honduras	Spain
El Salvador	Italy
Costa Rica	Switzerland
Panama	Morocco
Colombia	Saudi Arabia
Venezuela	Tunisia
Ecuador	Senegal
Peru	South Africa
Bolivia	Nigeria
Chile	Southwest Africa
Argentina	Australia
Brazil	Turkey
Paraguay	Greece
Uruguay	Portugal
French Guiana	Thailand
Surinam	Philippines
Dominican Republic	Malaysia
Haiti	India
Trinidad-Tobago	Pakistan
Jamaica	Oman
Bahamas	Norway

Fake "Porsche Design" and "Papillon" sunglasses like those shown above are popular items whether sold as "frankly" fake or the real thing.

England	Sweden
France	Finland
Northern Ireland	

Main supplying countries for fake or copied watches, sunglasses, jeans and other designer fashions:

Taiwan	Hong Kong
Korea	United States
Martinique	

Countries to smuggle gold or currency from for profits:

Mexico	France
Italy	Jamaica
Soviet Union	Poland
Bulgaria	Romania
Hungary	Yugoslavia
South American countries	African countries

| Central American countries | Socialist countries |
| Middle Eastern countries | Far Eastern countries |

Smuggling of untaxed currency to secret accounts in these countries:

Bahamas	Guernsey Islands
Panama	
Cayman Islands (be careful here)	
Switzerland (be careful here)	

Cayman Islands accounts are being penetrated by the United States Internal Revenue Service. Switzerland is also cooperating with the U.S. government.

Main countries where taxes are to be avoided or underground economies flourish:

United States	Iran
Canada	Saudi Arabia
England	Nigeria
Zaire	Cameroon
France	Ghana
Australia	Senegal
Spain	Honduras
Italy	South Africa
Guatemala	Zimbabwe
Mexico	Kenya
Colombia	Algeria
Venezuela	Ivory Coast
Bolivia	Somalia
Argentina	Angola
Brazil	Pakistan
Surinam	Afghanistan
Paraguay	India
Uruguay	Burma
Soviet Union	Thailand

Poland
Bulgaria
Turkey

Malaysia
Chad
Greece

Countries to smuggle guns to for high profit:

Mexico
Guatemala
El Salvador
Belize
Honduras
Costa Rica
Panama
Colombia
Venezuela
Guyana
Brazil
Ecuador
Peru
Bolivia
Chile
Paraguay
Argentina
Surinam
Haiti
Dominican Republic
Jamaica
Grenada
Barbados
Bahamas
Trinidad and Tobago
St. Lucia
Dominica
South Africa
Southwest Africa
Indonesia

Somalia
Uruguay
Angola
Zaire
Zambia
Mozambique
Zimbabwe
Uganda
Sudan
Ethiopia
Central African Empire
Libya
Chad
Nigeria
Mauritania
Algeria
Liberia
Equatorial Guinea
Upper Volta
Lebanon
Turkey
Iran
Afghanistan
Pakistan
India
Bangladesh
Burma
Thailand
Malaysia
Northern Ireland

Philippines	Italy
France	Germany

Countries from which one can buy weapons:

United States	Spain
Brazil	Korea
Taiwan	West Germany
Portugal	

Countries to which one can smuggle drugs, thus earning easy profits:

United States	England
Australia	West Germany
France	Italy
Ireland, Northern Ireland	Canada

Main suppliers of illegal narcotics:

Marijuana	**Cocaine**
Colombia	Bolivia
Mexico	Brazil
Jamaica	Colombia
Guatemala	Peru
Panama	
United States	**Heroin**
Belize	Thailand
Thailand	Burma
Ghana	Laos
Togo	Mexico
Ivory Coast	Iran
Cameroon	Afghanistan
Turkey	Pakistan

Countries from which people can be smuggled for huge profits:

Haiti	Mexico

Colombia

El Salvador

Jamaica

Bangladesh

Dominican Republic

Venezuela

Argentina

Bolivia

Ecuador

Vietnam

Cambodia

Bahamas

Main countries that receive illegally smuggled people:

United States
Canada

Money, it's a gas
Grab that cash with both hands and
make a stash.

Dark Side of the Moon
Pink Floyd

5. Stashing the Cash

WHAT TO DO WITH THE MONEY? WE all wish we had such problems, but cash flow to smuggling networks chokes life from their system.

Today the IRS, Customs, and all the other agencies who make up government opposition are after the underground money. They simply want to use these billions of dollars for their own inflated overspent budget. Now, you don't think they burn it, do you? Hell no, they employ more people with it. It is a circular scenario where illegal subterranean money pays for government. In reality the government doesn't want smuggling to go away, for it pays a huge segment of their bills and employs thousands of people. Stop smuggling all together and some one hundred thousand government employees of federal, local and state institutions lose their jobs. Millions of dollars in equipment would lie idle, rusting and unused in various parts of the world.

We are all told that we must put money to work. Invest it, bank it, buy real estate or whatever. This is excellent for a corporation, but smugglers cannot follow this rule without a real fear of detection. The following rules are more suitable for smugglers.

- Don't invest anything over fifty thousand dollars in a U.S. venture on a legitimate basis.

- Bank in the United States in increments of seventy-five hundred dollars or less.
- Don't use tax lawyers. Many of these people are constantly yet quietly monitored in the United States.
- Never deposit foreign bank checks in a U.S. bank if you're a smuggler.
- Use cash for most of your material purchases.
- Use several different banks in nearby towns. This allows you more flexibility.
- Store your cash in various places, not bank safety deposit vaults, but private safety deposit vault centers. These are springing up all over the good old U.S.A.
- Have numerous credit cards and use them. It is best to *always owe* money to some institutions.
- Use foreign banks for only a portion of your cash. Never wire money. Use the dress codes as previously outlined and do your own banking.

One of the main objects in money markets is to let your cash work for you, but smugglers must realize this cannot always be their way of life. They should spend their cash with vigor and not worry about prevailing interest rates. Cash must always be trickled into any institution, as any large deposits are immediately subject to scrutiny.

It is best always to pay taxes on a small portion of your income. One cannot drive around in fancy sports cars and live in $450,000 homes on a $30,000-a-year salary. Be very practical in this area.

The middle of the road is where the white line is—and that's the worst place to drive.

Robert Frost

6. For Our Own Good

PERHAPS THE BEST WAY TO BEGIN this chapter is to say that law enforcement agencies have the power of Goliath. They have the ability to break the law in order to save the public—and often use it. While house burglaries, murders, rapes, and other crimes of violence go almost unchecked, smugglers are pursued with vigor. Pick up any paper and see that murderers, rapists, and other sundry folk will pay bonds of one thousand to ten thousand dollars for their violence while smugglers, who are generally nonviolent, will be issued bonds that run from one hundred thousand dollars to figures well into the millions. Most law enforcement people have all the funds and resources necessary to mount quite formidable operations against citizens. They are all wired into a multi-phase crime computer system known as NCIC—National Crime Intelligence Computer. This little bear can gobble up information on people fast. It also can spit out facts and whatever hearsay or speculation people decide to program in.

Municipalities

These boys are usually fairly well trained, poorly paid, and of average to good intelligence. The larger the city, the larger and better equipped these scouts usually are in today's world. A word of advice: don't conduct a smuggling operation in your home city. Always work in cities miles away. You'll often find that one city won't cooperate with another due to petty rivalry.

County Sheriff's Office and State Police

All county sheriffs have their organized crime bureau, generally known as OCB. The county usually has more highly paid and often better educated personnel than the city has. Anywhere from ten to twenty-five people constitute an OCB unit, which generally researches bullshit offenses. They are underpaid but have close ties to federal authorities. Feds and county police love to work together, but locals and feds kind of dislike and distrust each other. There are now tons of multiagency strike forces made up of all kinds of people who act together and exchange information. Generally they're after druggers, but under the new Racketeering Influence and Corrupt Organizations Act (RICO), even parakeet smugglers face large losses of property and no-parole prison terms.

Forget the state police unless you get caught for traffic offenses.

Federal Government

Personal vendettas appear at this level. Lots of personnel, money, and wasted time appear at this level. The federal agents all work at the same level and get a meager check. The Drug Enforcement Administration may be the most corrupt unit here, but IRS is now pushing for the lead. Since Uncle Sam can claim what he wants and has the investigative tool of the grand jury on his side (a kind of legal corruption exists here—we'll call it the prosecution's family), this is a very dangerous scene. Remember the government loves to be tough and cold with all its captives. Never, but *never,* give the government help; it *always* backfires. Just pay taxes and be a good old boy.

The Internal Revenue Service

It should be understood that the Internal Revenue Service is vastly expanding its intelligence operations because of the U.S. underground economy. The new IRS special intelligence unit will watch money flow through banks and other cash institutions. In essence they will be watching money and paper. If you follow our rules, no paper will exist for the IRS to follow.

Along with this paper-watching, the IRS special intelligence unit will go undercover to "sting" people, or, in the Abscam scene, create a crime to catch the vulnerable. The IRS unit suspects that between $32 billion and $75 billion goes untaxed each year.

The new IRS unit will include the following:

- An integrated intelligence network, capable of being computerized and able to extract data from numerous other government computer data bases. The IRS will work with the Drug Enforcement Administration, the Federal Bureau of Investigation, the Securities and Exchange Commission and, of course, Interpol. Members of the special intelligence unit now have access to secret bank accounts in the Cayman Islands, the Bahamas, Switzerland, and the Guernsey Islands off the coast of England. IRS sources revealed to us that this will give the agency a clearinghouse approach to all important IRS data on U.S. citizens.
- There will be a greater use of undercover operations. This will be done to explore the now existing tax shelters.

- There will be broader and more sophisticated "sting" operations. This will be done to infiltrate areas where large amounts of cash pass back and forth. Watch out for the IRS, they just purchased a large order of video taping equipment.
- There will also be a much broader use of search warrants by IRS agents. IRS informants will be wired with body microphones so that conversations will be recorded. (These are easy to detect.)

It is easy to see that almost everyone will become a target of the Internal Revenue Service's Special Intelligence Unit. Sophisticated corporations can hire good lawyers to tie down IRS investigators for years. Unfortunately, you and I cannot do this, so we become easier targets. Everyone from waitresses to flea market merchants can be popped, so protect yourself. We have explained how to protect your cash. Remember to keep it out of the "paper trail" that the IRS will follow.

The Federal Bureau of Investigation

These gentlemen are still in the J. Edgar Hoover image, but their newer agents are better than the old-timers. They are using many nonofficial deep cover people who work on the "outside" for years at a time. It is getting harder and harder to detect the outsiders, so we suggest polygraph tests for any suspicious people. They utilize body microphones a great deal in undercover work. These are concealed and taped to their side. Occasionally frisk your people at meetings to test them for microphones. Most agents are high caliber and professional by nature. Don't offer them money, because 99 percent of the time they are incorruptible. They are generally poor to mediocre combat shooters. They are mediocre undercover operatives, but they seem to be improving.

The Federal Drug Enforcement Administration

Quite simply, this is a bucket of worms. Quality of some of their people is good, but a marjority are poor at best. More and more of their people are getting arrested with the criminals. Rumors of DEA corruption appear to be more factual as high-level agents are arrested. They can probably be bought at certain levels, but we would not recommend such action.

Friends of ours within the DEA state that their unit's reorganization, currently underway, could improve operational ability. They have many obstacles to face, and there is some infighting with local police. In general, they are good shots and live by the Starsky and Hutch image.

Some of the best DEA office units are:

- Fort Lauderdale unit headed by Frank White. White is honest and tough. He left the Miami office after being accused of killing a smuggler. This occurred July 31, 1980, in Miami. He has been the subject of numerous inquiries, but he comes out clean. Don't mess with this unit.
- Miami office. The sheer numbers working for this office and the George Bush Task Force overwhelm you. They concentrate on the Keys and the south Dade County areas known as the Redlands. They've had good success against Latins, but a bad record against the "good ole boy" smugglers of south Dade and the Keys.
- New York City office. This group comes in third place. For years dope slipped past up here and French Connection stashes disappeared, but that is over, gang. The New York troops are finally serious.

Some incidents of DEA unresolved cases are:

CREDIT: WORLD WIDE PHOTOS

This false gas tank was used to hide loads of smuggled cocaine. Obviously, the plan was not executed perfectly.

- An unannounced inspection of a DEA office turned up fake signatures on DEA forms used to account for payments to informants. Six agents had access—case unresolved.
- One drug defendant claimed an agent stole $9,300 from him. Agents found money was indeed stolen—case unresolved.
- An agent stationed in Mexico falsified his travel vouchers so he could travel to the United States and buy guns. He resigned.
- A drug defendant claimed he sold over $4,000 worth of heroin to a DEA agent. The agent was dismissed.
- A south Florida DEA agent was arrested for making obscene phone calls. He retired with a reduced pension.
- A senior DEA agent was indicted for smuggling. He was one of the top agents on the George Bush Task Force. His case is pending.

These are only a few of the infractions which occur, but it shows the drug problem. The best drug agents appear to be local enforcement units. DEA often gets credit, but our hats go off to the following top local units in the United States:

- Fort Lauderdale's narcotics unit run by Nick Navarro. Don't fool around here, gang. You'll fall hard.
- Palm Beach County's multiagency Narcotics Task Force. Made up of many small city personnel, this unit has been involved in busting some biggies.
- Tampa, Florida's Hillsborough County Narcotics Unit. Sheriff Walter Heinrich may be the best at his job in the United States.

CREDIT: WORLD WIDE PHOTOS

Photo shows bundles of confiscated marijuana being guarded in front of an AWAC radar plane known as EC-121.

- Honorable mentions go to Orange County, California, Harris County, Texas, San Diego, California.

The Central Intelligence Agency

This is a nonpolice agency. They have no police powers, and agents generally dislike any association with other federal agencies. The quality of operations personnel has slipped badly over the past five years. Most of the real quality young people have left for greener pastures.

It was the old-timers who taught smuggling to the Cubans. The old Miami-based "J. M. Wave" program was the experimenting ground for today's Latin smugglers. But one must remember that our government is allowed to let its own intelligence services smuggle if it serves government interests.

U.S. Customs Service

These people are capable, but overall their quality is low. Generally they like to bust dopers and gun-runners, but they actually get few quality smugglers.

Alcohol Tobacco Firearms of U.S. Treasury Department

This is the end of the line as far as U.S. agencies go. Their main thing appears to be harrassing gun shops. The whole agency may even go down the tubes in the months ahead. They generally hire lower caliber people, and no wonder. I mean, who'd want their job?

To sum it up, the government at all levels has the money and investigative tools to indict Jesus, but if you've lived according to the rules in Chapter One, your NCIC printout will work for you, not against you.

You can fool most of the people, most of the time.

P.T. Barnum

7. Watching Them Watching Us

Cops ARE COPS, AND IF YOU SUSPECT problems, always check your rearview mirror. Cops like to remain two cars behind you. Always check for a police VHF antenna on a plain, drab, non-whitewall-tire car, generally a Ford or Chevy Nova. Cops always seem to appear as something they are not. Starsky and Hutch are not reality.

If you suspect surveillance, make a series of silly evasive turns. If still followed, do a 360 degree turn in behind the suspect vehicle. Write down its color and license. Later, drive by the police stations in the area and check to see if the car is there. We'll call these dog-fight tactics. Feds use all types of confiscated cars for their work, but they usually have the standard VHF antenna wire somewhere. Always check the federal enforcement lots to see what cars are in the allocated government slots. This is the beginning of your police intelligence dosier. Don't let the police be the only ones in the intelligence business. Begin to put them on the defensive, for they are doing the same to you. Remember that there is strength in knowledge. The more you or your people can detail on law enforcement's strengths, the better you are and the more precise your operation can become.

One must remember that cops have to make arrests to survive, for, like corporate executives, they are judged on numbers. Bust as many as possible and hope for the best result is their philosophy. Few bureaucrats read the conviction sheet, only the arrest sheet.

On surveillance, police usually have at least two vehicles: a prime car with one or two officers, and a backup. The backup is used when the prime has to drop off in order to appear less suspicious to the person being followed. Always make mental notes on cars behind you.

Women police officers don't look like Angie Dickenson; they have a sort of mean look in their eyes at all times. Generally, they are women who wish they were men. Some are attractive, but watch their eyes. They're cold, and they get involved in police work to build their egos. They are usually poor combat shooters and slow on the overall surveillance process.

Remember, if you're suspicious of surveillance, please make several series of evasive turns and maneuvers, always taking mental notes on the types of vehicles following you. Check for antennas and two-man that is, two men in the front seat. Police call this little act "trade craft."

Federal agents often use disguised vehicles like Sears vans and garden nursery pick-up trucks. Sears vans are everywhere, but be suspicious if you believe yourself a target.

When meeting a contact always be the one to choose the meeting site. Don't let someone else be the person to choose. Drive around checking for secure sites where surveillance would be hard to carry out.

Remember Abscam? Well, the good congressmen and senators were all lured to a meeting place picked by agents. The surveillance was in a TV screen, just taping away. A pro would never have made that mistake. Never divulge the meeting place until just before the assigned time. Always arrive early and hold sensitive conversations outside in the open air. Carry a small spectrum monitor in your pocket in order to detect R.F. body bugs.

Here is a list of good countermeasure electronic equipment and equipment manufacturers:

- Dektor Spectrum Monitors made by Dektor Corporation of Savannah, Georgia. Weak on low-band frequency.
- Tactronix Corporation, located in Palo Alto, California, is into miniaturizing everything. This company builds good surveillance intelligence equipment.
- Technical Services Agency of Maryland also builds a good spectrum monitor.
- Mason Corporation of Fairfield, Connecticut is another good company with a fine line of equipment.
- We do not recommend Communications Control Company. Their overall line of equipment performed very poorly in our field tests.
- During equipment testing, we found that high-impedence or low-impedentce phone taps were difficult to find. We therefore recommend that all security level phonecalls be made from pay phones with a trusty pocketfull of quarters. Phone-masking equipment used to attack oscillators in microphones is easily defeated with line filters.

Personal security phone codes between you and your contacts should be established. Common sense should dictate how you work this out. Voice scramblers are not recommended because this is retrievable infor-

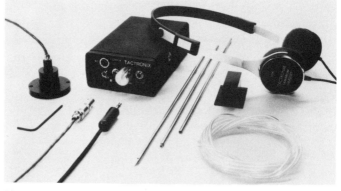

Various types of electronic audio surveillance equipment, as shown, is used by both sides of the smuggling game.

This audio noise jammer is used by smugglers to protect themselves against audio surveillance transmitters. It is also used by government intelligence case officers.

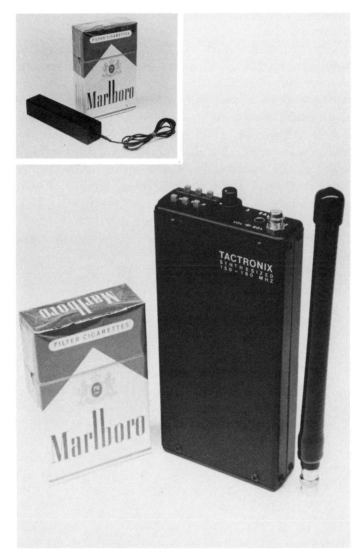

This state of the art synthesized pocket receiver monitors smugglers using "snitches" and room bugs. The insert shows a transmitter "bug" putting out 50 MW of power with a range of half a mile. This system is used by many of the world's government intelligence agencies.

mation which can be deciphered in today's computer-oriented society.

Bearcat Electronics makes a simple, inexpensive synthesized receiver. You can put it in your car and monitor any federal or local police frequency. Bearcat will also provide you with a list of all frequencies in your area. If you want to see what the police are doing, just punch in and listen. Some police intelligence frequencies are secret, but park near DEA offices at night and use the scan mode. Watch agents come and go and then follow some. Police, federal agents, anyway, almost never check for surveillance. We tried this experiment several times—worked great.

Police frequencies for your scanning are listed below.

Federal agents in Miami: this appeared as a tracking frequency for vehicles.

- VHF—between 171.450 and 172.200. Several frequencies appeared, including 171.600 and 172.000. These could be FBI, Customs or DEA. These frequencies are also voice channels for federal agents and appear to be national frequencies. Tests in Los Angeles, Orlando, and Miami showed these were one and the same unit.
- Other federal frequencies are:
  171.825
  165.2875
  166.4635
  170.4125
  167.4125

Remember, all frequencies are registered with the Federal Communications Commission, and almost anyone can research and obtain the police frequencies of federal agencies. Bearcat Electronics will also provide a com-

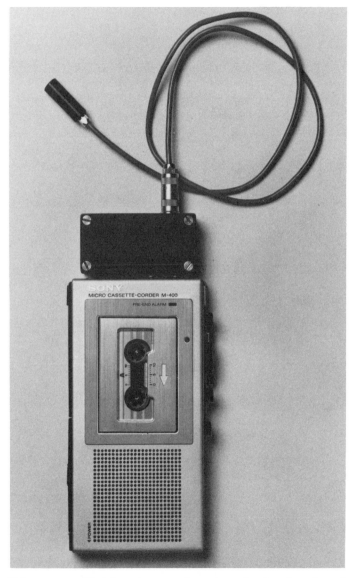

This power-amplified Sony tape recorder and remote microphone is used for police surveillance.

plete list of known frequencies for your scanning pleasure.

It will be important to use your Bearcat scanner to full advantage. With a scanner you have the ability to monitor all government frequencies. You might check a company called Digitcom, Box 1175, New York City, New York 10009. Digitcom will give you a full report on just how to expand your scanner. The report will enable you to look at all the "top secret" frequencies. There is also a book by Tom Kneitel called *Top Secret Registry of U.S. Government Radio Frequencies.* All the frequencies we previously reported are listed in Kneitel's book.

For a complete book of police radio frequencies write to: Hollins Radio Data, P.O. Box 35002, Los Angeles, California 90035.

Perhaps the most important comany you'll need is Hamtronics, Inc., 65 Moul Road, Hilton, New York 14468. Hamtronics manufactures an adapter to the scanners that allows you to receive:

72-76 MHz
135-144 MHz
240-270 MHz
400-420 MHz
806-894 MHz

These are very important for you to use in smuggling operations. The converters cover one single band each. Hamtronics will send you a full report and all information on each unit. This will give you a full capability between the frequencies of 30 and 512 MHz.

CRB Research, P.O. Box 56, Commack, New York 11725, can also send you equipment to expand your scanner units.

List of codes for police scanning:

Code 2	Accident
Code 4	Accident (Injury)
Code 6	Aircraft Crash
Code 8	Assault
*Code 10	Assist Other Unit
Code 12	Burglary
Code 12A	Burglary in Progress
Code 14	Forgery
Code 16	Dead on Arrival
Code 18	Dog Bite
Code 20	Domestic Trouble
Code 22	Drowning
Code 24	Drunk
Code 26	Fight
Code 28	Fire
Code 28A	Bomb Activated
Code 28B	Bomb Threat
Code 28C	Bomb Located
Code 30	Gambling
Code 32	Homicide
Code 34	Juveniles
Code 36	Larceny
Code 38	Missing Person
Code 40	Man with a Gun
Code 40A	Man with a Knife
Code 44	Officer in Trouble
Code 46	Prowlers
Code 48	Rape
Code 48A	Sex Offenses
Code 50	Robbery
Code 50A	Robbery in Progress
Code 52	Shooting
Code 56	Stolen Car
Code 58	Suicide
*Code 60	Suspicious Person

*Code 60A	Suspicious Car
Code 62	Traffic Detail
Code 64	Vandalism
Code 66	Jail Break
Signal 1	Contact Sheriff
Signal 3	Contact Deputy (Chief)
Signal 5	Contact Headquarters
Signal 9	Investigate Complaint
Signal 15	Warrants
Signal 21	Prisoner
Signal 25	Return to Headquarters
Signal 35	On Patrol
Signal 55	Civil Defense Alert

It is important to use clear frequencies for all your communications. There are certain areas within the spectrum that can be used free of government monitoring. These are areas that should be explored by smugglers because communications are so important to success.

"Mad" Mike Hoare needed clear communications for his failed mercenary attack on the Seychelles Islands. He and the South Africans set up a long range HF service running on 6.5219 and 16.5902 MHz. This HF band between 2 and 26 MHz is used by amateurs, marine boat captains and others for simplex purposes. The area between 2 and 22 MHz is maritime simplex and used by many scammers.

2.065 MHz	12.4292 MHz
2.079 MHz	12.4323 MHz
2.0965 MHz	12.4354 MHz
4.125 MHz	16.5871 MHz
4.1436 MHz	16.5902 MHz

4.4194 MHz	16.5933 MHz
6.2186 MHz	22.124 MHz
6.2216 MHz	22.1271 MHz
6.5219 MHz	22.1302 MHz
8.2911 MHz	22.1333 MHz
8.2942 MHz	22.1364 MHz

The 26 to 28 MHz is the CB band. This area is thought to be bad, but equipment is available, easy to use, and less crowded than most people believe.

The frequencies of 40.68 MHz and 27.120 MHz and 433.92 MHz are voice-free frequencies. These would be good and free of monitoring by government agents. Other short-range frequencies that would be good for use are the following:

- 50-54 MHz—6 meter amateur band; mostly SSB, some CW and FM.
- 57-72 MHz—TV channels.
- 72-76 MHz—This line of frequencies will be of definite interest.
- 76-88 MHz—TV channels.
- 88-108 MHz—FM broadcast radio band.
- 136-138 MHz—Space channels and microwave, almost all nonvoice.
- 138-144 MHz—These are important for smugglers because the military uses these channels for voice transmissions, especially in Florida.
- 174-216 MHz—TV channels.
- 216-220 MHz—Telemetry.
- 220-225 MHz—Amateur 1 1/4 meter band, mostly FM via repeaters.
- 225-400 MHz—This is good for smugglers because all the military aircraft use this to communicate with other aircraft. The aero-voice mode communications in this band are AM mode and can be of major interest.

- 400–406 MHz—Telemetry.
- 406–420 MHz—This is all government communications and is of major interest.
- 806–894 MHz—Metropolitan land bandmobile. This has been carved out of the UHF-TV channels.
- 406–410 MHz—This is an important area for all smugglers to monitor closely.

There are five VHF frequencies set aside for communications on intership traffic at sea. These are used on the water and are primarily for horsing around. Seldom do ships use call signs. These frequencies are sometimes used by clandestine eavesdroppers at inland areas away from ship traffic simply for their accessibility and lack of traffic.

156.375 MHz

156.40 MHz

156.525 MHz

156.625 MHz

157.425 MHz

The "Archer-Space Patrol" handy talkie operating in the 49 MHz is a free-of-monitoring item, which is excellent for short range communications. Also 147.57 MHz is another fairly good VHF channel away from highways.

Drug smugglers have been noted using the frequencies just outside the high frequency edges of the 20 and 40 meter amateur bands. These are international in scope, with stations on land and at sea. This all appears to be amateur radio equipment.

Most police intelligence communications equipment is manufactured by Audio Intelligence Devices, a Fort Lauderdale-based communications equipment company. They build body bugs, telephone taps, phony electric outlet microphones, and tracking equipment.

Their "body bug" units come in one quarter watt and one watt output. Their small bug, called a TX-703, runs between 30-50 Mgh and is simply not up to today's standards.

Their tracking equipment is equally substandard. It is called a "birddog unit." The signal you hear is pulsed and often sounds like the children's game "Battleship." Sometimes voice is included as an override. The transmitter is usually painted black and is held in place under the vehicle by a magnetic plate. It is very easy to locate if you look. The antenna is about seven to ten inches long.

The receiving vehicle uses two magmount antennas. Any car with two parallel antennas a short distance apart should be scrutinized. The receiver tells you to turn left or right. The antennas could be built into a luggage rack on a van or car, but this is the exception rather than the rule. The unit can be put in planes, or even on boats, for tracking purposes. In boats look below the waterline, for these transmitters can be placed in watertight containers and placed on the outside hull of the vessel.

In airplanes some tracking devices are wired into the main wiring system behind the firewall. It takes a careful physical exam to locate these. The transponder of an aircraft is sometimes changed by the government so that the transponder will squawk a continuous code no matter what numbers are dialed on the face. This code is picked up by the air traffic control center, which signals police aircraft as to altitude, speed, direction, and location of the aircraft. Actually, transponders can be put anywhere on a plane, so physical searches are necessary. We have already identified the best in counter-surveillance equipment. This equipment can be used to detect most any RF signal. It does take experienced personnel to use the equipment effectively.

White noise generators can attack most of the RF (radio frequency) crystal control transmitters. These generators can be purchased for about $400 from Tactronix. Tactronix is now owned by Orion Electronics of San Jose, California. This is considered the premier intelligence electronics company.

Ocean Applied Research in San Diego, California builds an omnidirectional tracking system. The receiver antenna, similar to a television antenna, can be inside the van where it will not show. It is a single circular antenna which rotates seeking the transmitter. It is expensive and out of range for most police units.

One favorite surveillance tactic of DEA is to knock out one taillight of the vehicle to be followed. This allows the surveillance unit easily to trail the subject. To counter this, check your car each night. Surveillance tactics vary among different units, but there are basic similar activities. Surveillance is a long, tedious process undertaken by law enforcement and intelligence officers. It is easily recognized if one checks consistently for people and vehicles. Most good scammers use what are called spotters. These people watch the home, parking lot, cars, and places of business in order to spot surveillance units. In essence, they are a surveillance unit used to spot surveillance from opposition forces.

In summarizing equipment and law enforcement units, let's state two things. You can order Audio Intelligence Devices' catalog and all its equipment very easily. This is a fairly easy company to penetrate. Just get stationery made up with a police heading and a post office box like Bill Smith, Hunter County Sheriff's Office, P.O. Box 1700, Marshall, California. The post office box will actually be a mail forwarding unit. Put a telephone answering service to work answering your phone or use call forwarding. Have the answering service answer as "Sergeant Smith's office." This trick always works. Most other companies fall for this, too.

The second thing is that you must prepare yourself to face the opposition. You do this by learning all you can. Put them under surveillance and you'll pick up lots of data. Most successful major smuggling units have intelligence sections that do nothing but collect facts on federal operations. The saying may well be: an electronic ear for an electronic ear.

Countersurveillance Equipment

    Spectrum analyzers
    Spectrum monitors
    Frequency counters
    Telephone cloaks
    Telephone analyzers
    X-ray equipment for hardwire
    Frequency scanners

Microphones

A simple microphone hidden in a strategic location and connected by a long cable to an amplifier or tape recorder is the simplest type of effective bug. Such a system would be useful, for example, in a motel room if advanced access could be assured to plant the mike and run the cable. Such an installation requires considerable time to do professionally. Sensitive microphones less than a half-inch across and thin cable to match are readily available from the hearing aid industry. Such cables are delicate.

Special microphones called "spike mikes" can be placed through a wall to intrude into the subject's room. It is best to drill a hole and press the long mike tube through it. This technique permits listening without having to visit the suspect's room first. Even so, it is recommended that the spike mike be installed before the subject is present. It could be rather embarrassing if the startled suspect were to watch a drill bit suddenly pop through his wall.

Directional Microphones

Many experiments have been made in an attempt to develop sure methods of bringing distant noises closer: bird calls for nature lovers, concert hall sounds for audiophiles, news coverage by reporter teams, even huddle calls at football games. Two types of highly effective systems have emerged.

Parabolic Mikes

Parabolic microphones are awkward and not very effective. They work exactly like UHF-TV antennas: The incoming sound waves are reflected from the parabolic surface, focusing at a point. The microphone is mounted at that point. In addition to amplifying weak sounds from considerable distances, parabolic mikes are also very directional. Since sound sources located off to the side are not amplified, there is no interference with the desired voices. Such directional microphones are useful over hundreds of feet in range. Because of their size, it would be impossible to set up a two or three foot parabolic mike in a crowd without drawing considerable attention. For this reason, most parabolic mikes are situated in a nearby van or vacant room during active surveillance.

Shotgun mikes, or "rifle mikes," are not as wide, but they are quite long. Several feet of piping extends in front of the microphone, directing sound to the element. These mikes can be frequently seen mounted

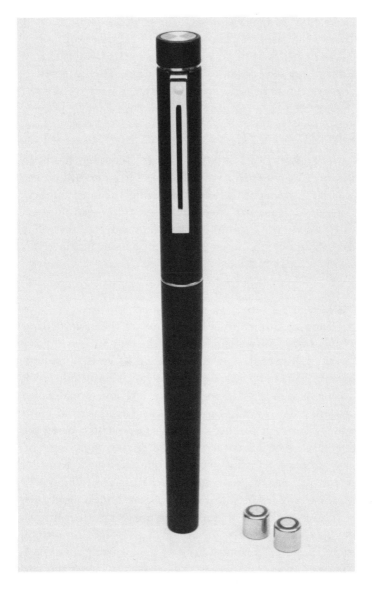

This pen transmitter is used primarily by police informants and government agents. Its range is up to half a mile.

above the audience in performing halls, and pointed toward the stage for audio pickup of the performances.

Both types of directional mikes cost several hundred dollars and have a limited application. They are generally used only when access by other means would not be possible.

Tape Recorders

The advent of miniature cassette recorders has been a boon to undercover surveillance. Virtually any of the popular tape recorders will work fine for most applications, and standard, two-hour tapes are readily available. Inexpensive miniature, pocket cassette recorders are usable when compactness is important. Pearl, AIWA and Tactronix make excellent units.

Telephone Taps

Tapping a telephone line is one of the easiest forms of electronic surveillance. Even the telphone company has on-line recorders which are used to verify customer service. These devices record for hours with large reels of slow-speed tape. Similar recorders are available for investigators as well. Tape time can be conserved enormously through the use of activating circuits. When the telephone receiver is taken off its cradle, there is a voltage drop on the line which is sensed by the recorder activator, and the tape begins to run. Vox (voice activated) switching is another approach, and is handy for concealed mikes. The tape does not begin to roll until the vox circuit senses noise, such as voices or normal room clatter. The only critical part of using a vox system is to make sure that the sensitivity and delay are properly set. Otherwise, the recorder may not start up, or perhaps some sounds will be missed. If too sensitive, the recorder will continue to run without voices, which wastes tape.

Telephones may be tapped a number of different ways. The simplest is an actual electrical connection to the customer service line itself. This may be made at the terminal block on a nearby utility pole, or even at the telephone exchange building. If it is inconvenient to listen personally or to leave an unattended tape recorder, a radio transmitter which relays the conversation to a remote point may be used.

The "infinity transmitter" or "harmonic bug" is a phone tap that may be monitored from anywhere in the world. *The agent must first install the unit on the suspect's telephone.* When he completes dialing the suspect's telephone number, just before the first ring should be heard, he blows into a harmonica. That tone activates the bug, which disconnects the ringer circuit in the telephone. At the same time, the mouthpiece is connected to a high gain amplifier. The agent may listen to any conversations in the vicinity of the telephone. Incoming callers would merely hear a busy signal. If the telephone is lifted from the cradle to be used, the circuit automatically disconnects, thereby restoring the phone to normal.

For less sophisticated applications, a replacement "drop-in" mouthpiece transmitter is available. Looking nearly identical to the original handset cartridge, the drop-in unit is actually a radio transmitter. Any conversations occurring over the telephone will be broadcast to a waiting radio receiver monitoring the call. It is powered by the voltage on the telephone line.

Another tool of the tappers is the automatic number recorder. Affixed to the phone line, a digital circuit can monitor the tones or voltage pulses which correspond to

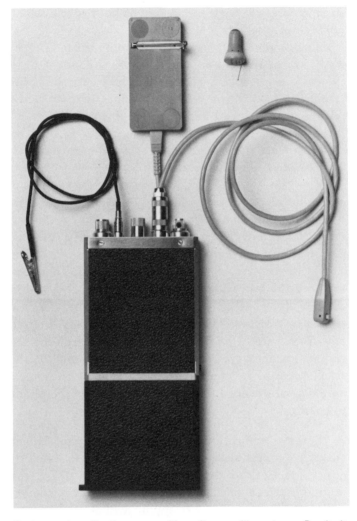

Pocket receivers like these are used by police surveillance teams. Despite its small size, it can collect enough evidence to put an unwary smuggler out of commission for a long, long time.

the telephone number dialed and display the corresponding digits as numbers on a panel.

The number recorder is an outgrowth of an instrument used by the phone company for many years which monitors the numbers dialed by a customer and prints them on tape to check on service.

Radio Transmitting Devices

While taps and mikes have a real place in intelligence investigations, most agents prefer to use miniature transmitters. Audio devices and radio transmitting equipment may be categorized with body bugs, room transmitters and tracking transmitters comprising the major divisions.

Body Bugs

A body transmitter is worn by the undercover agent. The device may appear to be a wristwatch, fountain pen, or even a shoe heel, but such imaginative applications have very limited range. In *nearly all actual applications,* the agent wears a cigarette-pack-sized transmitter strapped to his side. The units are commonly taped directly to the wearer's body and located under his upper arm. This location is least likely to leave a telltale bulge. The antenna is a flexible insulated wire, approximately a foot long. It is also taped to his body.

Because of the larger size of these transmitters, their battery packs are capable of supplying more power than those of tiny hidden transmitters. A range of hundreds of feet is routine.

Room Bugs

Among the more exotic devices are those manufactured for planting in the suspect's home or office, even in his car. To be effective, the transmitter must have long battery life and extended transmitting range, and be located where it is least likely to be discovered.

In an effort to disguise room transmitters, an endless parade of contraptions have been devised. They fit in wall sockets, lamp bases, picture frames and flower vases. They may be hidden behind drapes, under tables, within furniture upholstery, behind molding, or inside air ducts.

One advantage of transmitting devices which attach directly to electrically-powered appliances is that they may derive their operating power from the electric lines. These devices have an indefinite lifetime, and their transmitting range may be extensive.

High power and maximum range may seem to be ideal; on the contrary, high power can cause problems. For one thing, interference to the suspect's own TV and radio equipment may occur, *which is easily detected by countermeasures equipment.* Most hidden transmitters generate power in the 1/10 and one watt range.

Tracking Transmitters

When it becomes necessary to keep tabs on your vehicle, nothing is better than a reliable "bumper beeper." "Slap-on" units with powerful magnets are available to anchor inside the bumper or below the undercarriage of the car. Other units are available to mount internally; these take power from the vehicle's electrical system.

In both cases, the purpose of the transmitter is to emit a *steady stream of radio pulses.* The *mobile agent* can then track the device, using a receiver tuned to the same frequency as the transmitter.

Surveillance may, in some cases, be effectively conducted for distances of a mile or more depending upon the installation. Ordinarily, the agent's car is equipped with two short whip antennas. When the suspect's vehicle is dead ahead, both antennas receive the signal at the same time; the receiver is either quiet or else responds by displaying on a meter or light. When the suspect's vehicle begins to move or turn, the receiver indicates the change in position.

Bumper beepers are relatively large and heavy due to their internal batteries, and will fall off in rough terrain unless they have been very carefully mounted.

Frequencies

With the number of surveillance transmitters made for law enforcement and government agencies, it is not surprising that their signals may be found on a wide variety of frequencies. A few of the more popular ranges are listed below:

- 86-92, 108-110 MHz: These are the most common ranges for inexpensive bugs sold as "wireless babysitters" and "wireless mikes." Their popularity arises from the fact that they may be monitored with conventional FM radios which normally tune 88-108 MHz. In most cases, consumer radios may be tuned slightly outside that range, which accommodates reception of the little bugs. A minor adjustment of the receiver will allow even further off-frequency tuning. In virtually all cases, the little transmitters are not crystal controlled, allowing changes in frequency by a simple screwdriver adjustment.
- 150-174 MHz: Commonly called "VHF-high band," this range is the busiest part of the spectrum for two-way FM users. An agency can use existing receiving equipment to monitor a surveil-

lance device operating on a frequency already authorized for use by that agency. Crystal control is the rule for transmitters. Higher quality receiving equipment is synthesized and provides greater reliability and range.

- 30–50 MHz: VHF-low band is a common choice where maximum range is important. Some tracking transmitters are found here. The new 49 MHz license-free walkie-talkie band has potential for low-cost surveillance techniques.
- 406–420, 450–512 MHz: To be sure, the UHF band is less crowded, but surveillance equipment tends to go for a problem price in this range. Federal law enforcement agencies use the lower portion of this range, while local and state agencies use the higher range.
- 72–76 MHz: Originally intended for low-power signalling, this obscure band is also used for professional wireless microphone applications. It is occasionally used for surveillance.
- 27 MHZ: This is the Citizen's Band. Low-cost equipment is available, but with the myriad CB'ers sharing the air waves, its use for surveillance is obviously discouraged.

The Future

There are more fanciful surveillance devices in use. These are primarily concocted on a one-time basis by government intelligence agencies. The bug uncovered in the Oval Room of the White House during the Nixon administration was one example. The tiny cavity device discovered in the beak of the eagle at the American Embassy in Moscow was another. Laser monitoring of room conversations by reflections off window glass has actually been accomplished, but the costs are enormous.

Solar recharge of batteries is a novel approach to conserving energy, but it requires external wiring. "Free power," using the energy from nearby broadcasting stations to power a bug, is generally impractical. In all probability, the techniques which we have already described will be in common use for some time to come. Equipment will shrink in size as more and more components are miniaturized, and as batteries become more efficient; but no major breakthroughs in surveillance techniques for the police undercover agent seem near.

*I don't give a shit what
happens. I want you all to
stonewall it. Let them plead
the Fifth Amendment, cover up,
or anything else if it will
save the plan.*

Richard Nixon

8. Blocked in the Bushes

In 1981, PRESIDENT REAGAN WAS urged by the state of Florida's congressional representatives to set up a blockade to fight smugglers; that is, drug smugglers, weapons smugglers, people smugglers, and any other type that might frequent Florida soil. After consideration by Attorney General William French Smith and the heads of the different law enforcement groups within the Justice Department, a proposal for a military blockade against smugglers was created. This blockade would be named after our vice president, George Bush. There is great speculation as to why, but one law enforcement official told us that he believed Bush's name would add some guts and luster to such a creation. Or perhaps the actual reason for the addition of Bush's name is that our vice president has had millions of bureaucratic jobs, such as CIA chief, chief of the Republican National Committee, envoy to the People's Republic of China, congressman, and vice president of the United States—so why not "blockade chief"? Well, in reality, the purpose was simply to pit the military against the smugglers, and Bush's name was the key to military approval of the plan.

Today, such a blockade is known as a George Bush blockade, and those crafty little devils that beat this mess are called "blockade runners." Some twelve new Bush blockades are going to be set up to protect American citizens from smuggling horrors. The cost will be staggering, and the result will be minimal.

Let's explore the blockade itself. In reality, this so-called blockade has been in effect for over five years. All it has done recently is use our country's military planes and forces to aid in the struggle. Also, the Central Intelligence Agency has been technically involved with the blockade, and many new street agents have arrived in Florida. Many bureaucratic, administrative developments have occurred, but basically, all that has been achieved is the reinforcement of a blockade that was already in existence.

How does the blockade work?

Well, it is not terribly complex, but requires some simple examination. The nerve center of the system lies in the Miami Command Center, known as the MCC. This is run by the Justice Department and serves as a database clearinghouse. Names of boats, people, plane numbers, or generally anything, right or wrong, can funnel into this database.

Agents get assigned targets from the MCC and are broken into groups. Each group has its own leader. Individual agents working through snitches develop leads, set people up or do whatever may be required to make a case. Remember, this is the Uncle, and he survives on numbers, so cases must be made—good or bad.

This is the area where the blockade begins to break down. You see, snitches are usually dopers who have been busted and let off on the condition that they'll make cases for our Drug Enforcement Administration. Remember, these snitches get *paid,* and this is the Uncle, to whom numbers are very important, so most snitches must produce, lie or no lie. Most snitches have prison hanging over their heads, so only God knows how many of them lie under oath. Our research leads us to believe that over 50 percent of all snitches under government control have lied under oath at least once.

Even in the famous DeLorean cocaine case, affidavits filed show that the DEA's key snitch has lied under oath at least two times, and probably more. He was a paid government snitch who created a crime to catch a named, famous person. This is a typical government practice today because pressure is on to make arrests no matter what. Basically, snitches are whores who are out to save themselves no matter the cost to anyone else.

To continue with the blockade, we have a coordination point through which local police and feds coordinate their operations. The reason for this is that the feds have all the hardware for big busts and gunplay.

Now, we get into the hardware business.

Homestead Airbase houses the Customs/DEA airwing that chases incoming planes. Now, how do they spot these hummers? Well, first we have our Coast Guard. These boys have numerous vessels running standard patrols off Florida, the Bahamas and, in particular, the straits of Florida and the Windward Passage between Haiti and Cuba. Besides these vessels on constant patrol, there are U.S. military satellites that are photographing Cuba. Our intelligence and military satellites, called "Intelsats," now monitor all the ships being loaded along the Colombian Guajira coastal regions. These mother ships are tracked north until they reach U.S. or Bahamian waters. Then they are stopped and seized by our forces.

The United States Bush blockade also uses AWACS

radar planes to flay a constant pattern along the Colombian coast on up to Bermuda. These AWACS radar planes, known as EC-121s, are Boeing 707 aircraft with a huge radar mounted on the fuselage. They are based outside Oklahoma City and fly with some U.S. Customs officers right on board. They constantly search for suspicious aircraft targets.

Besides AWACS, two U.S. Navy E-2C Hawkeye mini-AWACS are used in the blockade. These are propeller versions of the larger AWACS aircraft. The Hawkeyes have a 200-mile radius target area and use three radar specialists per plane. These aircraft fly what are called figure eight patterns in the Caribbean off the Bahamas, and sometimes in the Gulf of Mexico. Once a target is sighted, these planes call in the U.S. Customs/DEA airwing units. First on the scene is usually a Citation jet with its own radar scanner or the new Falcon C-140 jet, also outfitted with its own electronics.

From this point, Huey Cobra gunships and fixed-wing aircraft from the same airwing are called in.

There is also a fixed balloon at Sugarloaf Key which is on a cable up around a thousand feet. This balloon also scans the Florida straits for planes.

One important factor is that the Customs Citation jet and the Falcon C-140 fly long oval patterns, mostly over Andros Island down to Great Inaqua on up to Walkers Key and back again. This gives them excellent coverage of the entry areas from the Keys to Melbourne, Florida.

My God, you say, how can anyone defeat this? Well, it really isn't all that hard, and we'll show you how.

First, down in the wild Guajira Desert on Colombia's north coast, mother ships are indeed loaded and the people there know they are photographed by satellite and will be tracked north. Many times throughout the fall harvest season, the Indians will load what are called "dumb loads" onto mother ships. A dumb load is one that the dopers want to get caught. It is loaded onto boats in plain view and then the dopers put out to sea, knowing they are bait. A dumb load is marijuana mixed with ground stalks and other poor, poor quality weed. It smells like dope, but you'd have to smoke a whole 50-pound bale to get high. When a dumb load is seized, the Coast Guard crew on the cutter *Dauntless* get all excited, and the Colombian crew members are arrested and sent back to Colombia. We all read of sensational seizures of 50,000 pounds, and so we know the blockade works, right? Wrong! Of the *Dauntless'* over 400,000 pounds of weed seizure, more than half has been comprised of dumb loads.

The reason for this is that when the Coast Guard, Navy and Customs get a fix on a boat heading north, it takes lots of equipment to track that ship. By dumb loading, smugglers tie up a lot of U.S. government equipment and they deliberately create weaknesses in the blockade wall. The dumb-loaded ship travels on a set course, thus pulling government vessels off their defensive positions, where smaller vessels sneak through. Dumb-loaded ships, sometimes several at a time, travel the preset route. They are followed by smaller vessels which stay tied up in Barranquilla or another port until loading time. Under cover of darkness, they move out to be loaded. Even with the satellite's infrared photography, darkness helps to disguise the work. The boats are loaded, then sent right back to port. They move out the next night and head the opposite way, perhaps toward the Bay Islands off Honduras. They then head up the Yucatan and up toward northwest Florida or Louisiana for offloading. The ships also head toward

This U.S. Coast Guard Cutter docked at Miami has been the Nemesis of many a smuggler.

These ordinary-looking shrimp boats are like those used to haul large loads of marijuana.

Aruba and run the islands north, staying near Puerto
Rico, and then up the eastern Bahamas, where they
dump their load on a predesignated island.

Sure, good loads get caught, but the percentage is
lower than one would believe. From the isolated
Bahamas, good loads are brought in by small, fast boats.
Some of these even act as decoys to draw the Coast
Guard vessels' attention, while good loads run the block-
ade.

Remember, blockade frequencies are available, and
these people who man the blockade do communicate a
lot. Get the trusty scanner and find the proper frequency to listen to.

Many a person has monitored the times that Customs aircraft leave Homestead Airbase. They fly constant patrols, just like the military, and these are not
hard to monitor. You can see the Customs DC-3 fly at
1,500–2,000 feet along Florida's east coast. It makes
about four north/south round trips a day, watching for
boats and planes from 4:30 P.M. to about 10:00 P.M.

It is always the best practice to fly under cover of
darkness.

The longer the flight of the aircraft, the greater the
chance of detection. Our research of planes revealed
that if a pilot drops down to about fifty feet off the
water, his chances of detection at night are very remote.
If you leave from Grand Bahama or Abaco, go to fifty
feet. Even the E-2C aircraft have trouble picking up
small aircraft like a Beech 33-A or a Cherokee-6. The
ADIZ radar will not lock on to you and, if you're
caught, it will be pure chance.

During early November 1982, the Customs Cobra,
a fixed wing aircraft of Customs, and a Navy E-2C went
after an incoming plane, an Aero Commander. It was

This plane was captured from careless, hapless smugglers.

The Bell Jet Ranger used by smugglers can land anywhere, anytime, with almost anything.

loaded and they knew it. The three government planes tracked the aircraft to a point near Belle Glade, Florida, but the pilot of the suspicious plane knew he was being followed, so he went to treetop level. He was good enough to evade and lose three government planes. The next day the smuggler's plane was found in a crop duster strip. It had been burned by the pilot. All hands and the booty got away.

Remember one principle: the shorter the trip, the greater the chance of success. Stay low and fly fast.

Many times dumb loads are dropped over the coastal east Florida area by planes. When one hundred bales are sighted, Coast Guard ships, police, Customs and DEA all run to the beach area, and many small planes sneak through the blockade during the five- or six-hour commotion that develops. Decoys and dumb loads are the main techniques used to beat the system.

Sometimes at night, three small twin-engine aircraft will fly close together entering U.S. airspace. Then they head in separate directions to beat the blockade. If one is seized, the chance is 33.3 percent that it will be the hot plane. This is another decoying technique.

A friend decided to run numerous tests against the blockade recently in order to test its effectiveness.

The first test was done in a Beech Sierra. In broad daylight, the plane flew from Lantana, Florida, to Treasure Cay, Abaco. The altitude was 1,000 feet out to Abaco, flying time under two hours outbound. The aircraft flew without a flight plan. After one hour on the ground, it flew back at 100 feet above the water, just after dark. Using no lights, it flew directly to a rural airstrip in Palm Beach County. There was no flight plan and no problem. The same plan was carried out flying in a Cessna 172; the return was in daylight to the Palm Beach Gardens Airport—no Customs, no flight plan, no problem. On over ten separate occasions, tests beat the blockade without any effort.

A friend in a DC-3 repeated a coastal entrance in daylight—no problems. It was decided to try this effort on a boat from Bimini. We encountered no Customs, no anything, but we did get a hard look from a Coast Guard plane, and later watched two Coast Guard boats without a hitch. By the way, we were in a thirty-foot Scarab Sport with over 470 horsepower in the engines. We averaged about forty-eight miles per hour on our return run. This was repeated at night by several friends and no problems were encountered.

We decided then to select certain targets within the blockade and keep them under surveillance and see what happened. The results were phenomenal. Shortly we were led to homes, addresses, and government targets without even a slight chance of being discovered.

In Houston, we found out a grand jury witness was really a government snitch put in the grand jury room to solicit data from others brought in to testify. Later, we found she was even having sex with some of her federal control agents. Other unbelievable practices by agents were discovered. This is called countersurveillance, and is done all the time in the intelligence business. The data received from this countersurveillance will wind up sinking a major federal probe. Black bag jobs and other corrupt practices by government personnel were amazing. The funny thing is, it all started as a simple experiment to look closely at those who wanted to hurt some suspected people. Government abuses are rampant and generally go far deeper than juries perceive.

In the Houston case alone, the main prosecutor (federal) had a longing for a woman in Washington, D.C. Federal agents had a female snitch tape phone conversations at their order, with no warrants. This female

Going down, as this plane did, makes the occupants "sitting ducks" for whomever is looking for them ... if they survive the crash.

snitch received government money and even falsified some data at the request of U.S. officials. She was paid and laid by government agents. It must be a good life, that one with old Uncle Sam.

Let us take the case of Teddy Feely, a special FBI agent and expert at black bag surreptitious entry break-ins—all in the line of duty, of course. To defend us, he had to steal data. Did he work on any blockade targets? You can take it to the bank. Well, the only problem was that Mr. Feely has been indicted for bank robbery and credit union theft, and numerous other charges await him from two separate grand juries. Since Feely worked against Eastern European targets as well as blockade targets, chances are he'll walk free with a slap on the wrist. The reason is, he worked with the CIA's counter-intelligence staff on some breakins, and that data won't make its way to court. Our objective here is to show that, in even the most sensitive areas, our government agents are extremely vulnerable to crime. Feely could face up to fifty years in prison, and he may represent only the tip of the iceberg—if indeed he is even judged guilty.

In yet another incident of blockade failure, U.S. Customs Special Agent William Logan of Miami stated in late November 1982, that the U.S. Customs Service would conduct a massive investigation into corruption within the U.S. Customs Service. Apparently, Customs agents have been paid off to allow suspected drug money launderers the freedom to move huge sums of money across our shores. Both U.S. Customs and Bahamian Customs agents have been suspected and implicated in this new probe.

We have already shown the massive problems within DEA, so one must look and see the tremendously weak links within the blockade infrastructure. There are many problems at the local enforcement level as well, so cracks exist all over the Bush blockade system.

One major point of the Bush blockade is fear. It creates an illusion that the area surrounding Florida is invincible. The illusion is good for those citizens who fear the awful problems associated with smuggling and piracy, and it justifies tax dollars, but it is also totally false. Much of what is seized is dumb loads, and many hot loads pass without even a twitch. Much of the new violence associated with the blockade is actually a by-product of the blockade itself. Another new phenomenon associated with the blockade is the appearance of huge homegrown marijuana crops in Florida, Georgia, North Carolina, Virginia and, of course, the Pacific Northwest. Now we have a multibillion dollar blockade to protect our national peace of mind, and the booty is being grown at alarming rates on our own soil.

In Florida alone, marijuana is more profitable than the entire citrus industry. In the mountains of Tennessee and Carolina it has replaced moonshine and brought new life to a troubled economy. Out in California, well, that crop is higher in value and pure dollars than California wine production and vegetable production together.

Intermixed with this, Jordache jeans, Rolex watches, and all types of other counterfeits are coming from the Orient undetected by West Coast agents.

Even Russia's blockade has failed to halt counterfeit jeans and watches. In Moscow alone, according to the newspaper *Socialist Industry,* one group of counterfeit blue jeans operators was arrested for selling $65 Soviet jeans for $240 a pair after putting on Jordache and Calvin Klein labels.

The newspaper went on to say that these counterfeit dealings often go on in public lavatories between youngsters. Real designer jeans may often sell in Moscow for over six hundred U.S. dollars. Just pack your suitcase with designer jeans and have a ball in Moscow's lavatories.

In a secondary part of the blockade, Colombia has orders to shoot down, not force down, unauthorized U.S. planes entering Colombian airspace. The number of U.S. civilian planes shot down is unknown, but according to Guellermo Jeja, a Colombian Air Force intelligence captain, that number is high. Most of the well-connected Colombians can easily get you past the Colombian mini-blockade, but go unprotected and down you go. By the way, the United States finances all the Colombian air operations aimed at drug interdiction.

In some cases, seized U.S. planes in Colombia have been reseized by U.S. operations experts. A small group from Boca Raton, Florida, have been most effective and are probably the world's leaders at international repossession of boats and planes. They are also experts at aiding people in foreign prisons and have an excellent track record in this area.

Blockade Summary

To beat the Bush blockade, remember several key points. Whatever you may be carrying, don't enter the United States on a single trip. Don't travel from pickup point to home direct. It can be done, but your risk factor greatly increases. Use a good drop-off point in the Bahamas or Belize or some other host port. The laws in these host countries are usually a lot less severe than in the United States. Also, host countries can easily be bought. We have already seen the corruption in the United States. Just imagine what it is outside of here. It is called *mordida,* and it works.

These wrecked planes never made it home. Neither did the smugglers who used them.

Always, but always, pretest your entry route and remember the dress codes. Most smugglers who are extremely successful do not look the part.

Always use countersurveillance as a way of life. know who you deal with or don't make a deal at all.

Remember, if you are caught entering Colombia illegally by air or boat without a visa, the small sum of 17,500 U.S. dollars sets you free. This is a misdemeanor in Colombia, but it could land you five years in a U.S. prison for something called "conspiracy." Just what that means nobody really knows, but the U.S. government loves to use it.

Smuggling Bibles from West Germany to East Germany can get you the death sentence, so everything equals out in the end.

Remember to keep your group of people small. The more people who know of you and your business, the more problems you have and the more weak links can appear.

If you are going to work by plane, use small craft like single-engine aircraft. Be inconspicuous. It is better to carry less and return to work another day than to be the bigshot multiton man. They mostly end up in jail.

The same rule of thumb holds true for boats. Large, fast boats are very visible. Go slow and do not be overloaded. Travel to the islands by day or night in groups of small boats.

Remember also to monitor the frequencies we gave you and to buy the necessary monitoring equipment.

The Bush blockade is looking to seize the obvious, so travel outside the parameters of the smuggler's image.

Chance favors a prepared mind. Reduce the risk factor to a minimum.

There is one more minor factor on the Colombian or Jamaican dope business. All loads can be insured, so if you lose one, no sweat—it's insured, and a good seller will get you another load for free.

Beating this system is not so difficult, but getting the courage to try is yet another story.

Courage is perhaps the single most important factor in beating the blockade. If you beat it once, you'll see it isn't all that tough to do, but it sure takes guts to push on and do it over and over. It is almost like the old Berlin blockade, but Americans beat that one, too.

Prohibition is yet another example of an unsuccessful blockade in past history. In the months ahead, many new Bush blockades will spring up in Texas, California, New York, Massachusetts and Atlanta. This will be done to bolster some of the original Bush blockade failures. Each area is unique and will require certain skills, but the blockade will be beaten, for it frustrates a need that customers want filled. If the price per chance is high enough, there will always be someone to try and make the run.

*Crime is contagious. If
the government becomes a
lawbreaker, it breeds
contempt for the law.*

Justice Louis Brandeis

9. Prime Examples

THIS CHAPTER WILL BE DEVOTED TO some of the major smuggling units that have fallen to defeat. By seeing what happened, one can learn from experience. They are the pirates of the modern world and, like Jesse James or Billy the Kid, legends will be written about these pirates years from now. These groups operated under such names as "The Black Tuna Gang" and "The Company," as well as "Steinberg's Machine" and "The Sunburn Group." They were all flamboyant, and in all cases they are in prison or have fled to Costa Rica, Aruba, Colombia, or other places.

They reached to the sky for cash, and they fell hard. Most are good honest people, all nonviolent, and all good citizens. They were lawyers, airline pilots, and salesmen, and what's more, all were smugglers. Their lifestyles and behavior devoured them. Even when they knew police were monitoring their every move, they smuggled. In all cases, they played their game too long, and in all cases believed they wouldn't fall. "A man has to know his limitations," said Harry Callahan.

The Black Tuna Gang

The exporting head of the Black Tuna Gang was educated at Tulane University and speaks perfect English. He lives in Santa Marta, Colombia, where he controls his own private army. His mother was once mayor of Santa Marta. Other members of his family were educated at schools in Florida. The gang drew its name from the radio code signal it used, "Black Tuna."

The government estimated that the Black Tuna Gang imported about 8 percent of all marijuana entering the United States. This estimate is absurd, and was done as part of a government publicity campaign against the Tunas. The U.S. connection for the gang was a small-time boy from Philadelphia. He and his partner are currently both in prison doing long, hard time. The main pilot for the gang made numerous trips to Colombia. He jumped bond and currently lives in Aruba on a yacht. DEA is still tracking him.

The group started out using aircraft, refueling at Cap Haitien, Haiti. They then flew on to a safe, after-dark landing at Santa Marta Airport. The plane spent one hour on the ground and left for the return, refueling at Cape Haitian. Their main landing site in Florida was Lake Placid Airpark. Homestead Airport was used, as were fields near the center of the state.

Through greed for more money, the group advanced to boats. They lost one load on a C-146 at Pahokee Airport, only because they got lost. They also used the Colombian Airport at Rio Hacha and one southeast of there.

For more than a year they were under surveillance by U.S. authorities, and they knew this, but they continued using their phones and conducted business as usual.

The connection made his original contact with the gang by flying on his own to Santa Marta, Colombia. This group still operates, and the gang's marketing manager has visited the United States many times illegally. The new Tunas run their booty to the Bahamas. All their refueling is done at Matthew Town, Great Inaqua Island, in the Bahamas. Small boats transport to the U.S. mainland. The group uses Andros Island for most offloading operations.

The Company

This was originally an Illinois and Missouri group looking for big bucks.

The Company was headed by a decorated Vietnam veteran who lost his legs in the war. A Colombian connection and others set up the operation abroad. The group kept some of their planes in Nicaragua under the Somoza regime. They used San Marcos and El Banco, Colombia, and clandestine strips near Rio Hacha on Colombia's Guajira Peninsula.

All the group's planes were procured by a Fort Lauderdale plane broker. Using DC-4s, DC-7s and DC-6s, the Company flew to their Colombian airstrips. Planes were stored in the Exumas, Bahamas, South Caicos, and Aruba for use. Planes landed at dusk and were fueled and loaded. They then headed north at night on a direct course to Haiti. They overflew Haiti at about nine thousand feet and began their descent over South Caicos Island. They lowered or descended to about twenty-five hundred feet and proceeded west of Nassau. South of Grand Bahama Island they descended to 100 feet and flew direct to the Fort Pierce/Stuart area. They entered the United States at the Fort Pierce/Stuart coast going over 200 miles per hour and at an altitude of 50 to 100 feet above ground. They entered the United States between 4:30 A.M. and 5:00 A.M. Once they were over land, they gained altitude where radar contact was made, but now they appeared as a plane just taking off.

Their favorite landing site was near Punta Gorda, Florida. An army of ground crews awaited their touchdown. A DC-7 was unloaded in about fifteen to twenty minutes. That is ten tons of grass.

The Company had all employees polygraphed. Their security started out good, and then fell apart. The leaders were warned they were under close surveillance fifteen months before their fall, but they refused to believe it. They made enormous amounts of cash, but their egos could not admit they would fall. They had access to the best intelligence in the world, but failed to believe it.

Today all members are in jail but two, who live in a villa near San Jose, Costa Rica, but frequent the Bahamas. Splinter units of the group still operate, using Cessna 404 Titans. This group was permier at buying airfields with local police protection in Georgia, Alabama and South Carolina.

The Boyd Brothers

The Boyd Brothers are ex-army and former Vietnam veterans. The one feat of the Boyds' was donating huge sums of cash to Jerry Lewis' telethon for crippled children. Estimates are that the Boyds gave over $150,000 to the telethon at various times. The Boyds were a split-off from another great dope ring where they got started unloading boats and planes. When the flashy leader got nailed, the boys took over the operation.

They employed a military airdrop specialist who, while in the service, coordinated all airdrops in the Florida Everglades. This became their trademark. One bale of marijuana was marked with a red "X," and inside was up to ten kilos of cocaine. No matter what happened, they always retrieved the bale with the X in order to make a profit. They were also the first group

Here's another mission foiled in the end.

to fly from Colombia using an entry point into the United States at a point south of Naples, Florida. The last 300 miles were done at about fifty feet off the water.

Both the Boyds got caught, jumped bail, and now live in Colombia near the town of Barranquilla. They also travel to Jamaica, a place they had good dope connections.

The Sunburn Group

The Sunburn Group operated out of Key West, Florida. It was run by an attorney known as "the President," who is the stepson of a Key West police chief. One Sunburn front was a legitimate suntan lotion business. This group imported using shrimp boats. It was considered a typical "conch" ole boy network. Their estimated importation was around three hundred million dollars; yes, that is *million*. The whole group fell because of a government snitch who supplied all vital data which put the men in jail.

The Delisi Gang

This was a father and three sons named Delisi. They put a connection together and imported using airplanes. Their downfall came when they recruited a prominent judge. The judge acted as a snitch.

The government chased the Delisis all over, finally catching them. Most of the brothers have jumped bond and are still working importing from Mexico. They live in New York City and Houston, Texas.

There are many more names, like a movie producer who was a huge mover of dope, utilizing boats. He had a Santa Marta, Colombia connection and operated for years. He imported to Long Island, New York, and to New England. There was a flamboyant doper who had connections to all the major rings. He is now dead, lost in the crash of his Mitsubishi II aircraft.

There are the pilots with literally hundreds of trips to the Guajira desert. There is the Zion Coptic Church, and oh, so many more. But the best success story is that of a forty-four-year-old from North Miami. He and his Cessna 172 make two trips a day to the Bahamas to pick up dope. He carries only 250 pounds, but each day that is 500 pounds. In ten years, he estimates he's run 500 trips without a hitch.

He lives comfortably, works alone, and flies in broad daylight. He will retire this year with about $20 million buried away. He has his wife and older kids now, so who cares about interest rates?

Death is not the greatest loss in life.
The greatest loss is what dies inside us
while we live.

Norman Cousins

10. And the Upshot Is . . .

W<small>E</small> HAVE TOUCHED ON MANY AS-pects of smuggling goods into or out of the United States. This phenomenon has gone through many ups and downs throughout history, but today smuggling is a middle- to upper-class disease. Basically, this upsurge from the criminal or lower-class problem to the middle and upper class has developed as a direct result of our own government's efforts. The U.S. government holds most of the responsibility in its own hands.

During the post-Korean War period, America developed a paranoia about Communism. Our government began to train indigenous groups to infiltrate and propagandize small Communist countries. The best example was Cuba in the late 1950s period, on into the sixties. Under the United States' "J. M. WAVE" program, we paid and trained and operated a small clandestine army to fight Castro. We taught people to smuggle, cheat and kill. We taught them how to set up safe houses and run small boat operations. We taught mother-ship operations, airdrop techniques, and camouflage.

By the late 1960s and early 1970s, the United States had changed policy. We were now more concerned with Asia and Vietnam, so we dropped our Latin operators and cut off the money. It was tough for our Cuban-

American brothers to go from ten years of being freedom fighters to being cooks or street cleaners. By pure
osmosis, these operators began to slip in small loads of
marijuana for community use. But by now it was clear
Vietnam was another of our defeats, and hippie and
yippie communities at all our major universities were
puffing up a storm.

Trained combat fighters from the Vietnam war were
coming home to an unwelcoming land. In Vietnam and
Asia, where dope was free, these men also sought out
the weed, and the market began to rise. During this
period, criminal penalties were small fines and a spank-
ing. The Vietnam veterans and the clandestine "J. M.
WAVE" personnel began to see the importation as fun
and challenging.

Many veterans began to see smuggling as easier and
more fun than being cooks or cab drivers. They mixed
with the bustling new Latin community of Dade
County. Their problem centered on the fact that they
were too successful and too good at their trade.

The U.S. government decided it had to get a piece of
the new money, or subterranean economy. By 1977
our government began to make new laws to curb the
flow by creating such things as the RICO Act, which
stands for Racketeering Influencing Corrupt Organizations. It allows the government to seize the material
assets of smugglers. This is to get a piece of the money
market, not to stop smuggling. What the government
did was create a situation where the price of the goods
goes up. In such situations money will be higher, allowing more smugglers a chance for greater profits. When
the smuggler is caught, the government will be able to
get more of material value from him. Hence, it is the
government pushing up the price on a weed that has a
market of over 50 million Americans. This is an upper-

and middle-class market that can pay the going rate. Our government pushes up the market, then literally waits to get more people willing to risk the run for phenomenal profits. On many occasions government officials will allow loads to get through safely so that they can eventually seize more of the smuggler's assets when they finally get him. Federal prosecutors call this "building a case."

A type of sickness begins to infect the government, which spreads to the smuggler as well. The entire system then becomes corrupt and devours whoever sets foot in it. In essence, it begins to look like the Vietnam war, but it is our brothers we fight, and our brothers and sisters who suffer.

Back in March 1980, the *Miami Herald* carried a truly interesting series on the city of Key West, Florida. This episode showed how a struggling area like Key West turned to the smuggling business for increased profits. It showed a town where smuggling touches literally everyone. It is a part of life in Key West, where police officials, lawyers, businessmen, public officials, and others have all been linked to the dope business. The docks of Key West are filled with "trippers."

One of the more interesting stories in the series on Key West was the one on Billie's Bar. It outlined how smugglers gave the owner of Billie's large sums of cash, and soon a partnership evolved. Billie's was supposedly renovated with drug money from an Atlanta smuggler. The bar increased its business, Key West prospered from tourists who liked to drink at such places, and the revolving door kept spinning. Visit Billie's in Key West and see how a little influx of cash helps a town in distress. Even Bobby Redfern, the president of the Key West Business Guild, says pot is Key West's biggest and by far most profitable business.

Knowing the techniques of evasive driving can save a smuggler from being caught by the cops *or* the robbers.

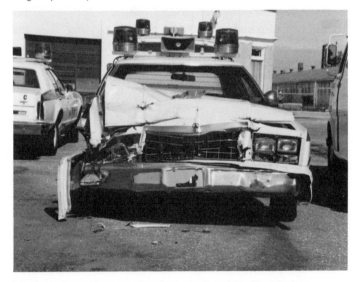

It's nice to know that sometimes even the "good guys" get theirs.

To illustrate our point on smuggling in the Florida Keys, we'll mention three things about justice there:

- Former Monroe County prosecutor Jeff Cautier compiled Florida's worst record on prosecuting drug felonies.
- Almost every multiton marijuana smuggling case prosecuted by the Monroe state attorney's office since 1976 has been botched, lost, or plea-bargained to misdemeanors.
- Almost all multiton offenders were allowed to plead guilty to possession of less than twenty grams, and they paid a small fine and went free.

We have reviewed many things in the book, but let's look again at the most important ones. Smuggling is a dangerous business and is not to be undertaken by squeamish or nervous people. An interview of one pilot who made a night trip illustrates that point:

We left Palm Beach Airport about 5:30 P.M. bound for Sandy Point in the Bahamas. Our Beech 36 could hold about one thousand pounds, and I was to get maybe twenty thousand dollars for the one trip.

The weather was not great, but me and the copilot headed direct to Sandy Point. The copilot put tape and sheets all over the cargo area so as no residue could get on the rugs of the plane or on the seats.

We flew at about two hundred feet over the water. We had our strobe lights on, and it was soon getting quite dark. Neither me nor the copilot knew anyone on the ground crew in the Bahamas, only knew they were black. They would hear us fly over Sandy Point, then radio us on a hand-held walkie-talkie on a VHF frequency. We would acknowledge, then make a U-turn to watch for their strobe lights, and land.

We approached Sandy Point in a small rain and damn, we could hardly see a thing. No lights, rain, and initially no radio contact. Well, some jerk calls on the hand-held, lights flick on, and shit, the rain starts dumping real hard.

Now I'm only 200 feet, so I swing around and see two strobe lights, one at one end and the other at the other end of what I assume is a landing strip. Well, we look at each other and say, "Let's go for it," so in we go.

We pull to a stop and maybe ten blacks greet us, and in seconds bales are being loaded. Guns are everywhere and old beat-up cars are carrying the booty. The booty is loaded in such a way that I know the plane is way overloaded. The lead black guy says maybe eleven hundred pounds, maybe a little more.

We begin our takeoff procedure and see that the man with the strobe lights has left and rain is pouring down. We are overloaded and cannot see the end of the runway. Off we roll, faster, faster. God, it seems like an hour. We rotate and get up slowly and over the water to fifty feet. All lights except the cockpit light are shut off.

Black, we can see nothing. Our altimeter says fifty AGL, which is fifty feet over the water at 133 knots. We hold steady in the rain—our eyes fixed on the instrument panel.

Flicks of vertigo snap at both me and the co-pilot.

Up ahead after an hour are two red dots. We both say ship, must be a ship. Then there it is. We pass over its stern. The Coast Guard, oh, damn, we laugh. We're scared, we feel lost, and we know that radios from the Coast Guard ship to shore must be banging out positions.

One sputter of the single-engine plane, and in the water we'd go—as there was no room for lots of survival gear. Occupational hazard, we both say aloud. Our minds are racing with fear, but neither of us is really nervous.

Soon there are the lights of shore, still at fifty feet. We are a little north of target, but no problem. We cross the beach north of Palm Beach and flick on all lights.

Destination: a crop duster strip west of Palm Beach. We make a series of evasive turns to look for surveillance or chase planes—none seen. We proceed to a small training airport and do two touch and goes and depart for destination. There it is, and we receive the all-clear from ground people.

We turn and flick off the lights and closer, closer—bang, we hit the ground. We stop—our hearts are racing now—we never turn off the engine in case we have to run. We toss out the goods, ground people help, and in seconds it's done and we depart. Throw out the sheets and tape and then clean the plane with a long hose like a pool hose. In the air, the air sucks out all the residue through the hose. It creates a vacuum and acts like a vacuum cleaner.

We head south to Homestead and land. A rent-a-car waits for us and down to the Ramada Inn for a few beers. The next day, it is home.

It is hard to describe it all: fear, fun, and it can be a hell of a thrill, to say the least. If you aren't scared, you're a real fool, but for $20,000 for six hours' work, why not do it twice.

Two nights later, out we go again, and man, you can lock yourself into that real easy, so I know it is time to quit soon.

I saw people scared and praying and I saw the real macho ones who aren't afraid, but they are the ones who are real dumb. A good healthy dose of fear can cure a whole hell of a lot of foolishness.

More than anything the copilot and I laugh about that Coast Guard cutter. We passed right off its stern, and it was just moving real slow northbound. I bet we scared hell out of one or more of the crew. I often wonder if they even cared or even bothered to radio in our position.

Two hours of darkness at fifty feet over the water takes its toll. You do earn the money, but it is a short-term business.

Let's review where to get started in the smuggling business. First, pick the product you wish to work in and then go out and develop a connection. Jordache jeans do well in Russia, but your initial expenses are high. Rolex watches from Switzerland are a good bet, but again expenses can be high at first.

If you have connections, say in Latin America, there is a need for products like guns, night vision devices, and tear gas guns. It is not illegal to sell those items in the United States, but it is illegal to ship them overseas. Hence, there is a ready market to buy them here and then sell them to a bogus company at a vacant lot or have them stolen from your warehouse. Happens all the time.

Counterfeit products like polo shirts and Cartier watches and Rolex watches all do very well in Latin America, and they are easy to smuggle in.

Relabeling of inexpensive California wines to make the bottle look like authentic expensive French wines is a new and profitable business. The funny part of this is that over 50 percent of all those who purchase the relabeled wines do not know the difference. They are buying a known name, a year, and a known vintage.

California and New York State are the places to start. One can buy large quantities of wine by the bottle unlabeled, and counterfeiting well-known labels is easy. Just stick them on and you're in business. Sell to your friends, and soon word will pass around, and a whole distribution network can be established.

It is our belief that Florida and Texas are the two best places to get into the smuggling racket. Key West or Fort Lauderdale are great places in the state of Florida to begin to seek connections. Any bar in Key West is a good place to start making connections, and Bootleggers in Fort Lauderdale is fine too. Even the Mutiny Club in Miami's Coconut Grove is a good place to visit.

Offshore in the Bahamas is another great place to visit and break into the business. It is also a good place for counterfeit jeans and polo shirts, and a great place for people-smuggling business. Hit Bimini first and go to Brown's Bar. Then the Anchor and Big Game Club.

Charge off to Nassau, but the real illegal action is on Andros, Abaco, Grand Bahama, the Berry Islands, Normans, Key, Great Inaqua, and oh, so many, many others. You have to pick yourself up and move out.

You will never get started by staying home in Des Moines, Iowa. You have to move out and make things happen as quickly as possible.

Remember the electronic equipment and the important radio frequencies, such as the following:

Federal Government

172.000	National frequencies
171.450	Voice and tracking
172.200	
171.600	
171.825	
166.4625	Mostly tracking gear
167.4125	
166.4625	
165.2875	
170.4125	

Georgia Local Police

Fulton County Police
171.6875
169.6875

Athens Police
156.7675
155.520
155.685

Cobb County Police
165.552
164.712

Atlanta Police
165.1875
172.950
155.700
154.950
173.300

Florida Local Police

Florida Keys (Monroe County) Police
167.4125
167.4215
167.9725

Miami Police
155.520
155.610

Fort Lauderdale Police
165.2125
165.1875
163.550
167.345

Tampa Police
167.0725
167.345

Royal Canadian Mounted Police

173.625   Mostly tracking
173.730
173.850
173.115

Immigration/Naturalization

170.775
170.700

Just scan the Bearcat through these frequency ranges because it is easy and each city has different frequencies. Spectrum analyzers will show on a screen what pulsed signals look like. Generally, the tracking pulsed signals are easy to spot or hear.

Radio watching and playing with the Bearcat scanners and spectrum analyzers are only a game that must be used in countersurveillance. The equipment is all commercially available and easy to buy. The more you practice these frequency search techniques, the more of a game it is.

Using a new Apple II and a home computer, we wrote a program to help us analyze equipment and store all frequencies. Most any frequency can be found and stored and retrieved at the touch of a finger. We are also now using the phone modem on the computer to get into some of the local police computers.

Just look through the police garbage. Usually access data is available. Computer bandits or pirates in California have a whole newsletter on how to do this technique.

Vince Lombardi of the famed Green Bay Packers said it best: "Keep it simple and execute."

Another simple rule that should be remembered is, "You become what you believe you are."

Smuggling should be a professional occupation for only a period of time. It is not a normal job and is set up for profits on an elevated scale. Even the famed pirate, Henry Morgan, quit being a smuggler pirate to become the British governor of Jamaica. The general philosophy is that if you stay in the occupation too long you stand a chance of a long fall.

Stay small, dress conservatively and open a small restaurant with your profits. Begin in the Caribbean where such names as "Morgan's Bluff" and "Smuggler's Cove" dot the hundreds of tiny islands and coves and intracoastal waterways. Don't stay in long and maybe you, too, like Henry Morgan, can become the governor of some plot of land. For behind every great fortune, you'll probably find a crime.

We have discussed types of transportation, such as smuggling by plane or boat. But what if you find you need to bring money into or out of the country? Where does it go? First, you must always adhere to the conservative business dress code: short hair, three-piece dark conservative suits, and wingtip shoes. This is all in the world of "trade craft." If you carry a cane which could be hollowed out, you'll look suspicious. We have carried almost anything in and out of the United States on dress code alone. Customs officials have a preconceived idea of what people who smuggle should look like.

Customs agents can check your bags, your briefcase, your cane, your cigars, but rarely, unless you really look awful, will they check your body. A good tailor can create many hidden pockets in coats or pants. Many documents and much cash can be hidden in these pockets.

I once had thousands in checks in a briefcase and placed them on top of the papers in the case. I laid *Playboy* magazine on top of the checks and two wet dirty handkerchiefs on the *Playboy*. I feigned a bad cold in line and sneezed near the Customs agent. Not wanting a cold, he waved me through in a hurry. Few people want to touch cold-ridden, wet handkerchiefs.

Don't overact. It takes some practice, but be conservative on most matters.

In cars, false-back seats are the standard hiding place. We suggest placing all the booty in tires, which are then filled with air. More cocaine, cash, and jewels have successfully crossed borders in tires than in any other car location. False gas tanks, dashboards, frames, and seats are the obvious search areas. The famed Bible smugglers of the world often place the Bibles in the frame or chassis. It should be understood that all religions of the world use smuggling techniques to spread the word. This is financed by big money, and it can be a profitable business. It can also be more dangerous than drugs and guns, but it is a fascinating business to research.

Don't be a wise guy and push Customs officials. Be conservative and use "yes sir, no sir" language. Work with them and say just what they want to hear. It is always best to operate through the system and not around the system.

One time, in carrying a special intelligence recorder-receiver system overseas, I loaded the tapes with heavy rock music. I knew I'd be stopped at customs with such a briefcase. When stopped and asked what it was, I simply pressed play and the system spoke for itself. The officials laughed as rock music blared out, allowing me to pass on through the customs barricades.

In most third world countries money talks loudest, along with the proper dress codes.

Within our world lies an abundance of smuggling opportunity. Whether you choose watches or smuggling money or gold coins from Mexico, each trip will be different and each will provide areas of fear, yet excitement. Pick your booty carefully, analyze your potential problems, and prepare your mind and body for the task.

The opportunity is yours, and "if you fill the unforgiving minute with sixty seconds worth of distance run, yours will be the world and all that's in it, and once more you'll be a man, my son."

Be careful—good luck!